Take It to Your Seat Centers

Math

4

Using the Centers

The 12 centers in this book provide hands-on practice to help students master standards-based mathematics skills. It is important to teach each skill and to model the use of each center before asking students to do the tasks independently. The centers are self-contained and portable. Students can work at a desk, at a table, or on a rug, and they can use the centers as often as needed.

Why Use Centers?

- Centers are a motivating way for students to practice important skills.
- They provide for differentiated instruction.
- They appeal especially to kinesthetic and visual learners.
- They are ready to use whenever instruction or practice in the target skill is indicated.

Before Using Centers

You and your students will enjoy using centers more if you think through logistical considerations. Here are a few questions to resolve ahead of time:

- Will students select a center, or will you assign the centers and use them as a skill assessment tool?
- Will there be a specific block of time for centers, or will the centers be used by students throughout the day as they complete other work?
- Where will you place the centers for easy access by students?
- What procedure will students use when they need help with the center tasks?
- Will students use the answer key to check their own work?
- How will you use the center checklist to track completion of the centers?

Introducing the Centers

Use the teacher instructions page and the student directions on the center's cover page to teach or review the skill. Show students the pieces of the center and model how to use them as you read each step of the directions.

Some centers have built-in scaffolding, offering more than one level of practice for the target skill. Carefully review each center beforehand to be sure that you are introducing or assigning the most appropriate level for each student or group.

Recording Progress

Use the center checklist (page 4) to record both the date when a student completes each center and the student's skill level at that point.

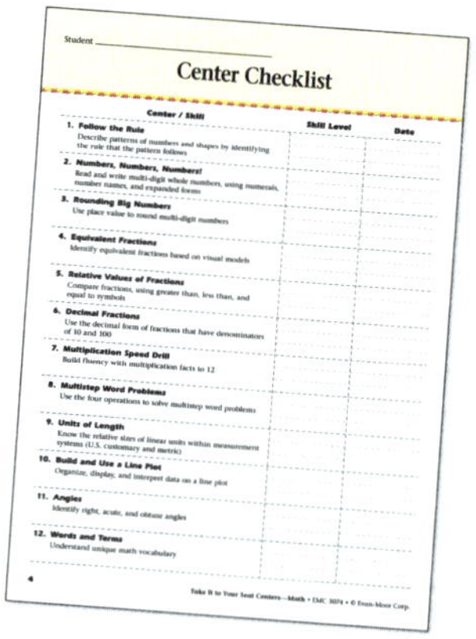

Making the Centers

Included for Each Center

- (A) Student directions/cover page
- (B) Task cards and mat(s)
- (C) Reproducible activity
- (D) Answer key

Materials Needed

- Folders with inside pockets
- Small envelopes or self-closing plastic bags (for storing task cards)
- Pencils or marking pens (for labeling envelopes)
- Scissors
- Double-sided tape (for attaching the cover page to the front of the folder)
- Laminating equipment

How to Assemble and Store

1. Tape the center's cover page to the front of the folder.
2. Place reproduced activity pages and a supply of scratch paper in the left-hand pocket of the folder.
3. Laminate mats and task cards.
4. Cut apart the task cards and put them in a labeled envelope or self-closing plastic bag. Place the mats and task cards in the right-hand pocket of the folder. If you want the centers to be self-checking, include the answer key in the folder.
5. Store prepared centers in a file box or a crate.

(A)

(B)

(C)

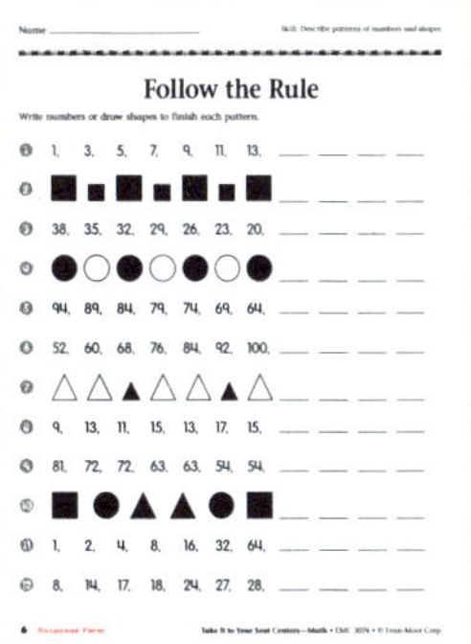

(D) Fold the answer key page in half, as shown. The answers for the mat activity are inside, and the answers for the reproducible activity are on the back.

Assembled Center

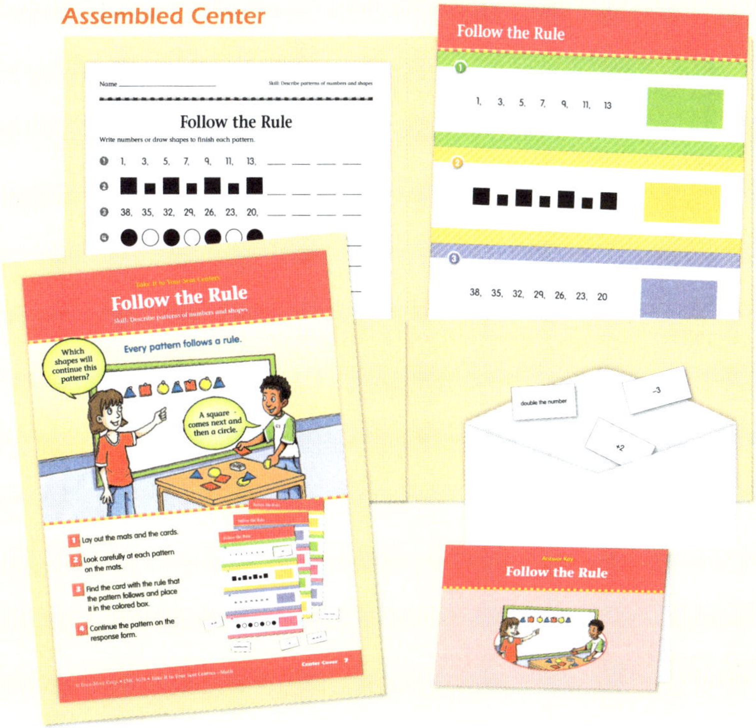

Student ______________________

Center Checklist

Center / Skill	Skill Level	Date
1. Follow the Rule Describe patterns of numbers and shapes by identifying the rule that the pattern follows		
2. Numbers, Numbers, Numbers! Read and write multi-digit whole numbers, using numerals, number names, and expanded forms		
3. Rounding Big Numbers Use place value to round multi-digit numbers		
4. Equivalent Fractions Identify equivalent fractions based on visual models		
5. Relative Values of Fractions Compare fractions, using greater than, less than, and equal to symbols		
6. Decimal Fractions Use the decimal form of fractions that have denominators of 10 and 100		
7. Multiplication Speed Drill Build fluency with multiplication facts to 12		
8. Multistep Word Problems Use the four operations to solve multistep word problems		
9. Units of Length Know the relative sizes of linear units within measurement systems (U.S. customary and metric)		
10. Build and Use a Line Plot Organize, display, and interpret data on a line plot		
11. Angles Identify right, acute, and obtuse angles		
12. Words and Terms Understand unique math vocabulary		

Take It to Your Seat Centers

Follow the Rule

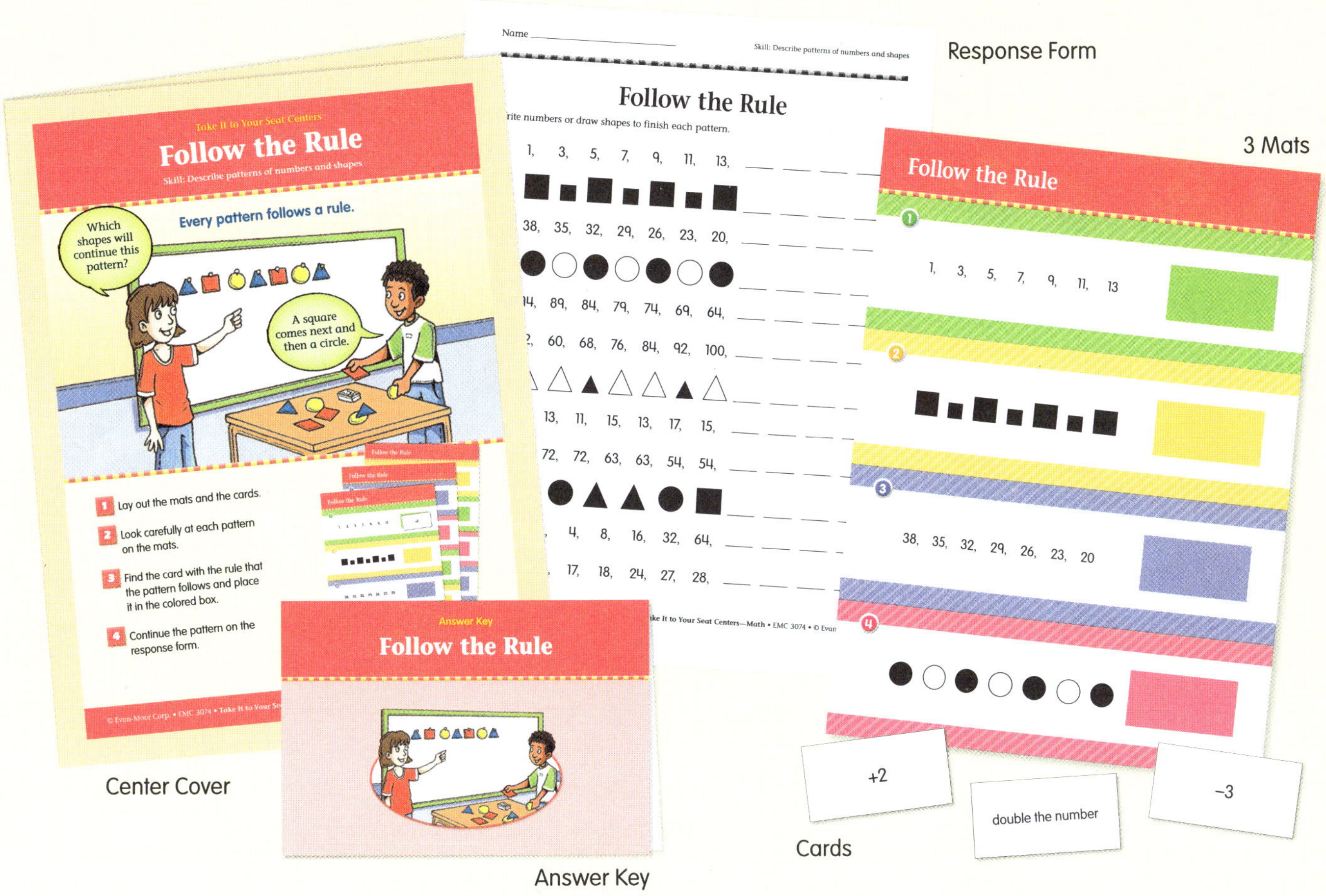

Skill: Describe patterns of numbers and shapes by identifying the rule that the pattern follows

Steps to Follow

1. **Prepare the center.** (See page 3.)
2. **Introduce the center.** State the goal. Say: *You will analyze each pattern on the mats to find the rule that the pattern follows.*
3. **Teach the skill.** Demonstrate how to use the center with individual students or small groups.
4. **Practice the skill.** Have students use the center independently or with a partner.

Contents

Follow the Rule

Write numbers or draw shapes to finish each pattern.

1. 1, 3, 5, 7, 9, 11, 13, ____ ____ ____ ____
2.  ____ ____ ____ ____
3. 38, 35, 32, 29, 26, 23, 20, ____ ____ ____ ____
4. 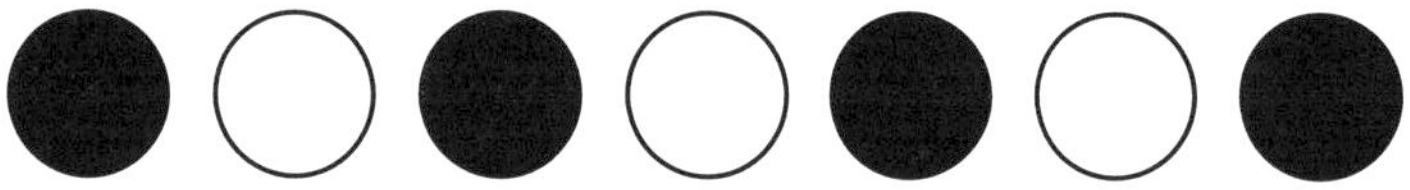 ____ ____ ____ ____
5. 94, 89, 84, 79, 74, 69, 64, ____ ____ ____ ____
6. 52, 60, 68, 76, 84, 92, 100, ____ ____ ____ ____
7.  ____ ____ ____ ____
8. 9, 13, 11, 15, 13, 17, 15, ____ ____ ____ ____
9. 81, 72, 72, 63, 63, 54, 54, ____ ____ ____ ____
10.  ____ ____ ____ ____
11. 1, 2, 4, 8, 16, 32, 64, ____ ____ ____ ____
12. 8, 14, 17, 18, 24, 27, 28, ____ ____ ____ ____

Take It to Your Seat Centers

Follow the Rule

Skill: Describe patterns of numbers and shapes

1. Lay out the mats and the cards.
2. Look carefully at each pattern on the mats.
3. Find the card with the rule that the pattern follows and place it in the colored box.
4. Continue the pattern on the response form.

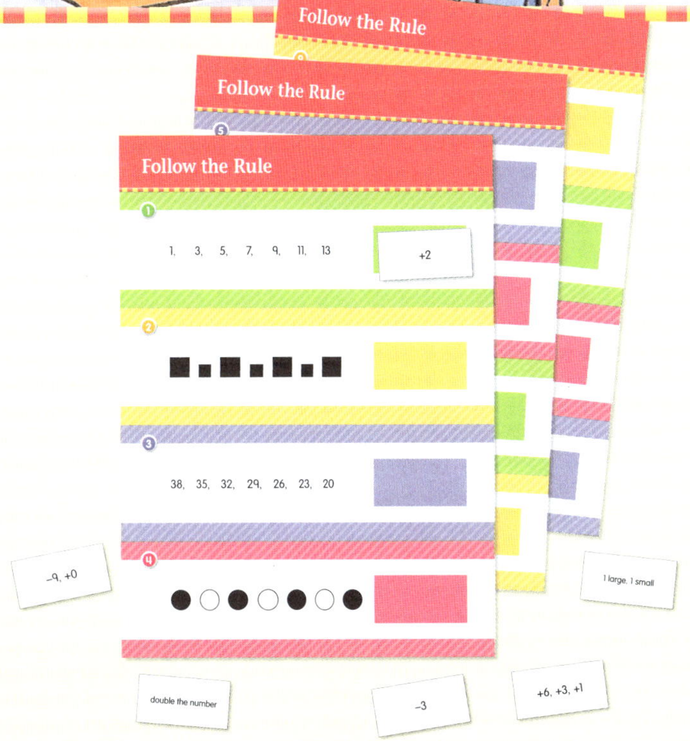

Answer Key

Follow the Rule

(fold)

Response Form

Follow the Rule

Write numbers or draw shapes to finish each pattern.

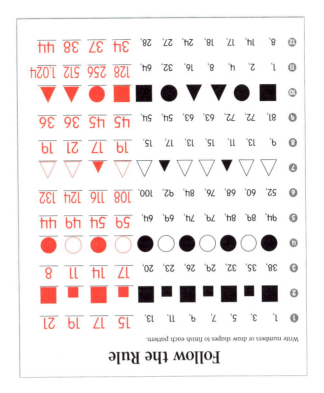

1. 1, 3, 5, 7, 9, 11, 13, 15 17 19 21
2. ■ ▪ ■ ▪ ■ ▪ ■ ▪ ■ ▪ ■
3. 38, 35, 32, 29, 26, 23, 20, 17 14 11 8
4. ● ○ ● ○ ● ○ ● ○ ● ○ ●
5. 94, 89, 84, 79, 74, 69, 64, 59 54 49 44
6. 52, 60, 68, 76, 84, 92, 100, 108 116 124 132
7. △ △ ▲ △ △ ▲ △ △ ▲ △ △
8. 9, 13, 11, 15, 13, 17, 15, 19 17 21 19
9. 81, 72, 72, 63, 63, 54, 54, 45 45 36 36
10. ■ ● ▲ ▲ ● ■ ■ ● ▲ ▲
11. 1, 2, 4, 8, 16, 32, 64, 128 256 512 1,024
12. 8, 14, 17, 18, 24, 27, 28, 34 37 38 44

Answer Key

Follow the Rule

Follow the Rule

1. 1, 3, 5, 7, 9, 11, 13 — +2

2.  — 1 large, 1 small

3. 38, 35, 32, 29, 26, 23, 20 — −3

4.  — 1 black, 1 white

Follow the Rule

5. 94, 89, 84, 79, 74, 69, 64 — −5

6. 52, 60, 68, 76, 84, 92, 100 — +8

7.  — 2 large white, 1 small black

8. 9, 13, 11, 15, 13, 17, 15 — +4, −2

Follow the Rule

9. 81, 72, 72, 63, 63, 54, 54 — −9, +0

10.  — square, circle, triangle, triangle, circle, square

11. 1, 2, 4, 8, 16, 32, 64 — double the number

12. 8, 14, 17, 18, 24, 27, 28 — +6, +3, +1

Follow the Rule

1

1, 3, 5, 7, 9, 11, 13

2

■ ▪ ■ ▪ ■ ▪ ■

3

38, 35, 32, 29, 26, 23, 20

4

● ○ ● ○ ● ○ ●

Follow the Rule

5

94, 89, 84, 79, 74, 69, 64

6

52, 60, 68, 76, 84, 92, 100

7

△ △ ▲ △ △ ▲ △

8

9, 13, 11, 15, 13, 17, 15

Follow the Rule

9

81, 72, 72, 63, 63, 54, 54

10

■ ● ▲ ▲ ● ■

11

1, 2, 4, 8, 16, 32, 64

12

8, 14, 17, 18, 24, 27, 28

+2	−5	−9, +0
1 large, 1 small	+8	square, circle, triangle, triangle, circle, square
−3	2 large white, 1 small black	double the number
1 black, 1 white	+4, −2	+6, +3, +1

Follow the Rule
EMC 3074
© Evan-Moor Corp.

Follow the Rule
EMC 3074
© Evan-Moor Corp.

Follow the Rule
EMC 3074
© Evan-Moor Corp.

Follow the Rule
EMC 3074
© Evan-Moor Corp.

Follow the Rule
EMC 3074
© Evan-Moor Corp.

Follow the Rule
EMC 3074
© Evan-Moor Corp.

Follow the Rule
EMC 3074
© Evan-Moor Corp.

Follow the Rule
EMC 3074
© Evan-Moor Corp.

Follow the Rule
EMC 3074
© Evan-Moor Corp.

Follow the Rule
EMC 3074
© Evan-Moor Corp.

Follow the Rule
EMC 3074
© Evan-Moor Corp.

Follow the Rule
EMC 3074
© Evan-Moor Corp.

Take It to Your Seat Centers

Numbers, Numbers, Numbers!

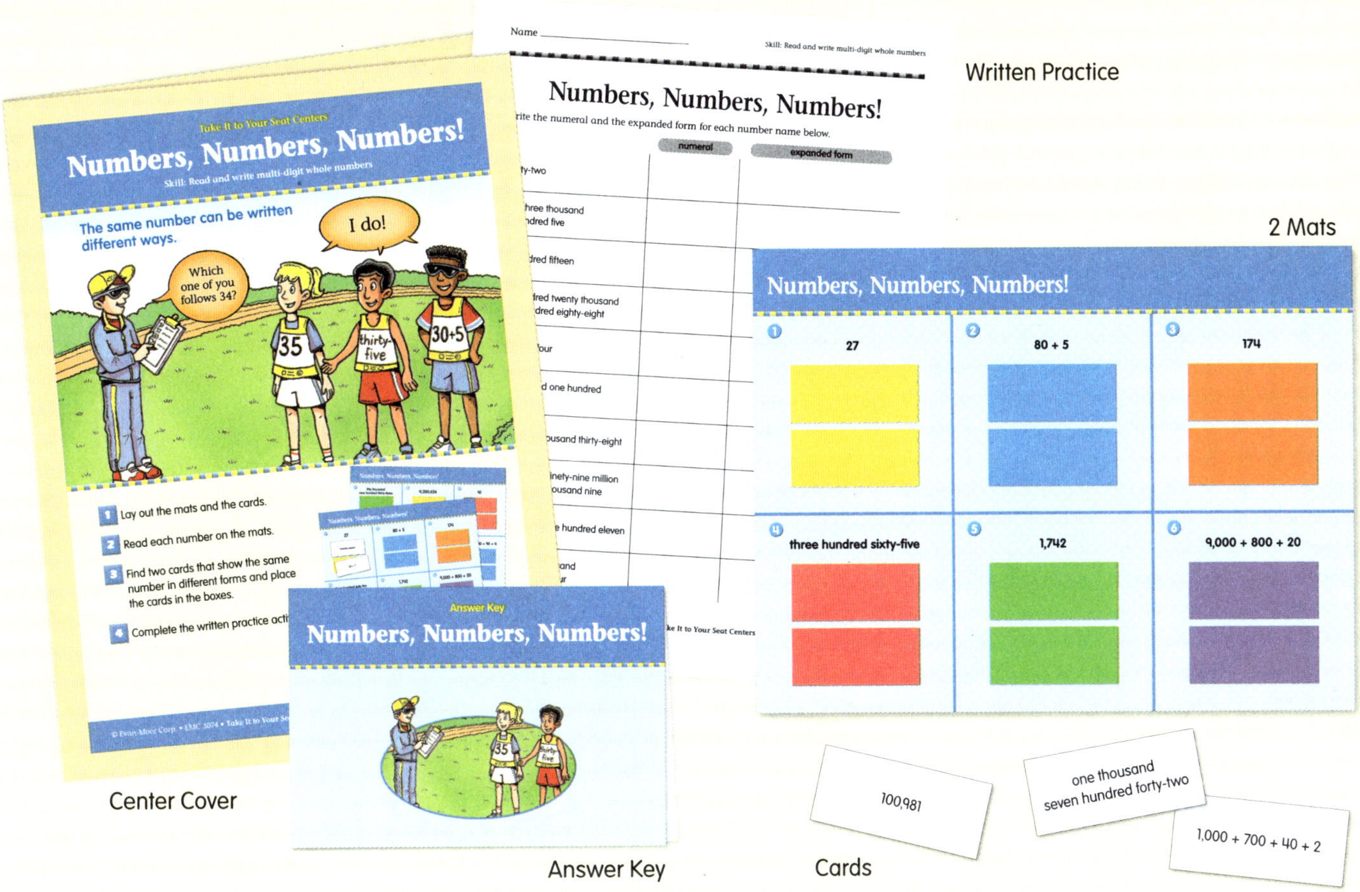

Skill: Read and write multi-digit whole numbers, using numerals, number names, and expanded forms

Steps to Follow

1. **Prepare the center.** (See page 3.)
2. **Introduce the center.** State the goal. Say: *You will find two other forms for each number on the mats.*
3. **Teach the skill.** Demonstrate how to use the center with individual students or small groups.
4. **Practice the skill.** Have students use the center independently or with a partner.

Contents

Name ______________________

Skill: Read and write multi-digit whole numbers

Numbers, Numbers, Numbers!

Write the numeral and the expanded form for each number name below.

	numeral	expanded form
ninety-two		
forty-three thousand six hundred five		
six hundred fifteen		
two hundred twenty thousand three hundred eighty-eight		
six million four		
five thousand one hundred thirty-seven		
twenty-two thousand thirty-eight		
nine hundred ninety-nine million nine hundred thousand nine		
one thousand one hundred eleven		
eighty-seven thousand six hundred fifty-four		

Take It to Your Seat Centers

Numbers, Numbers, Numbers!

Skill: Read and write multi-digit whole numbers

The same number can be written different ways.

1. Lay out the mats and the cards.
2. Read each number on the mats.
3. Find two cards that show the same number in different forms and place the cards in the boxes.
4. Complete the written practice activity.

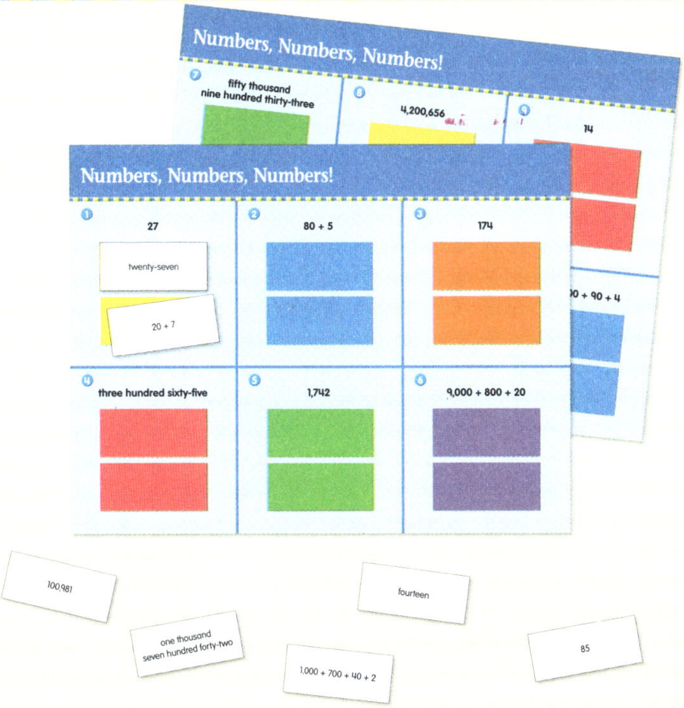

Numbers, Numbers, Numbers!

Answer Key

(fold)

Written Practice

Numbers, Numbers, Numbers!

Write the numeral and the expanded form for each number name below.

	numeral	expanded form
ninety-two	92	90 + 2
forty-three thousand six hundred five	43,605	43,000 + 600 + 5
six hundred fifteen	615	600 + 10 + 5
two hundred twenty thousand three hundred eighty-eight	220,388	220,000 + 300 + 80 + 8
six million four	6,000,004	6,000,000 + 4
five thousand one hundred thirty-seven	5,137	5,000 + 100 + 30 + 7
twenty-two thousand thirty-eight	22,038	22,000 + 30 + 8
nine hundred ninety-nine million nine hundred thousand nine	999,900,009	999,000,000 + 900,000 + 9
one thousand one hundred eleven	1,111	1,000 + 100 + 10 + 1
eighty-seven thousand six hundred fifty-four	87,654	87,000 + 600 + 50 + 4

Answer Key

Numbers, Numbers, Numbers!

Numbers, Numbers, Numbers!

1. **27**
   - twenty-seven
   - 20 + 7
2. **80 + 5**
   - eighty-five
   - 85
3. **174**
   - one hundred seventy-four
   - 100 + 70 + 4
4. **three hundred sixty-five**
   - 365
   - 300 + 60 + 5
5. **1,742**
   - one thousand seven hundred forty-two
   - 1,000 + 700 + 40 + 2
6. **9,000 + 800 + 20**
   - nine thousand eight hundred twenty
   - 9,820

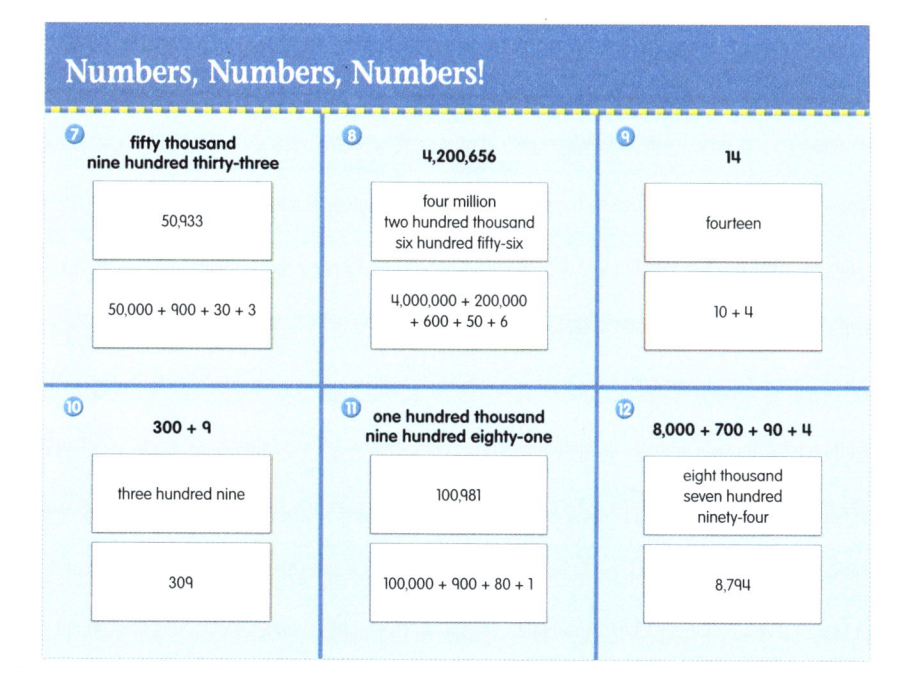

Numbers, Numbers, Numbers!

7. **fifty thousand nine hundred thirty-three**
   - 50,933
   - 50,000 + 900 + 30 + 3
8. **4,200,656**
   - four million two hundred thousand six hundred fifty-six
   - 4,000,000 + 200,000 + 600 + 50 + 6
9. **14**
   - fourteen
   - 10 + 4
10. **300 + 9**
    - three hundred nine
    - 309
11. **one hundred thousand nine hundred eighty-one**
    - 100,981
    - 100,000 + 900 + 80 + 1
12. **8,000 + 700 + 90 + 4**
    - eight thousand seven hundred ninety-four
    - 8,794

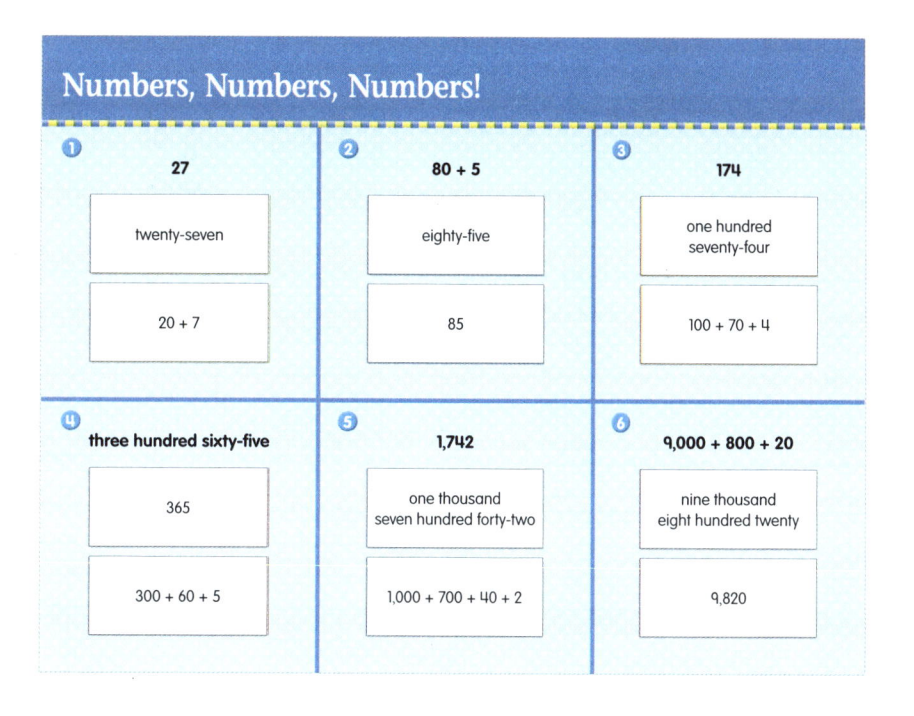

Numbers, Numbers, Numbers!

1. 27

2. 80 + 5

3. 174

4. three hundred sixty-five

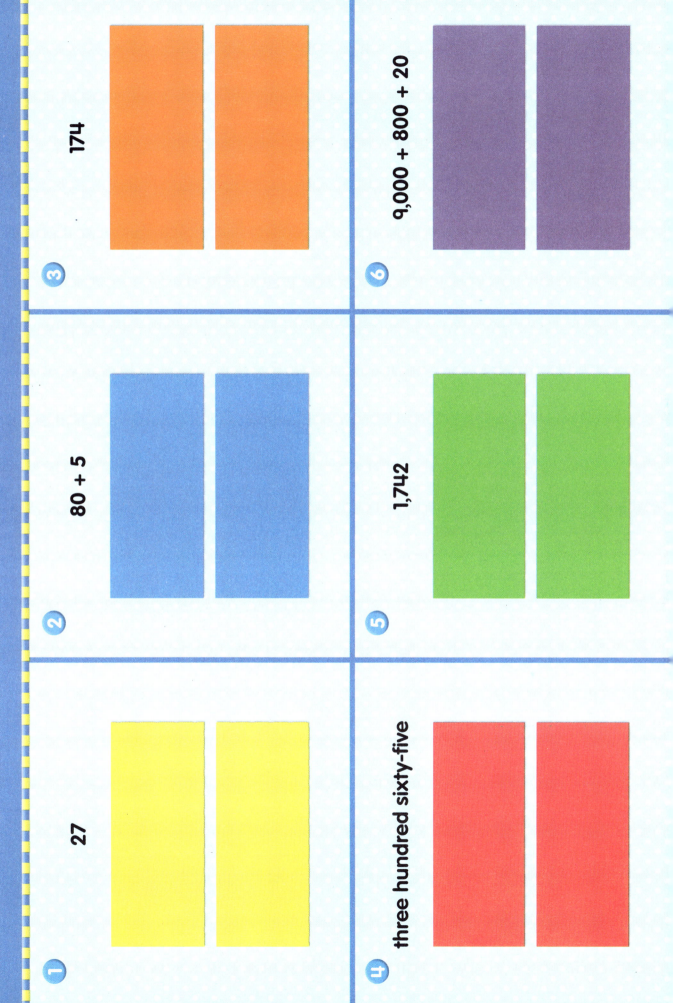

5. 1,742

6. 9,000 + 800 + 20

Numbers, Numbers, Numbers!

7. fifty thousand
nine hundred thirty-three

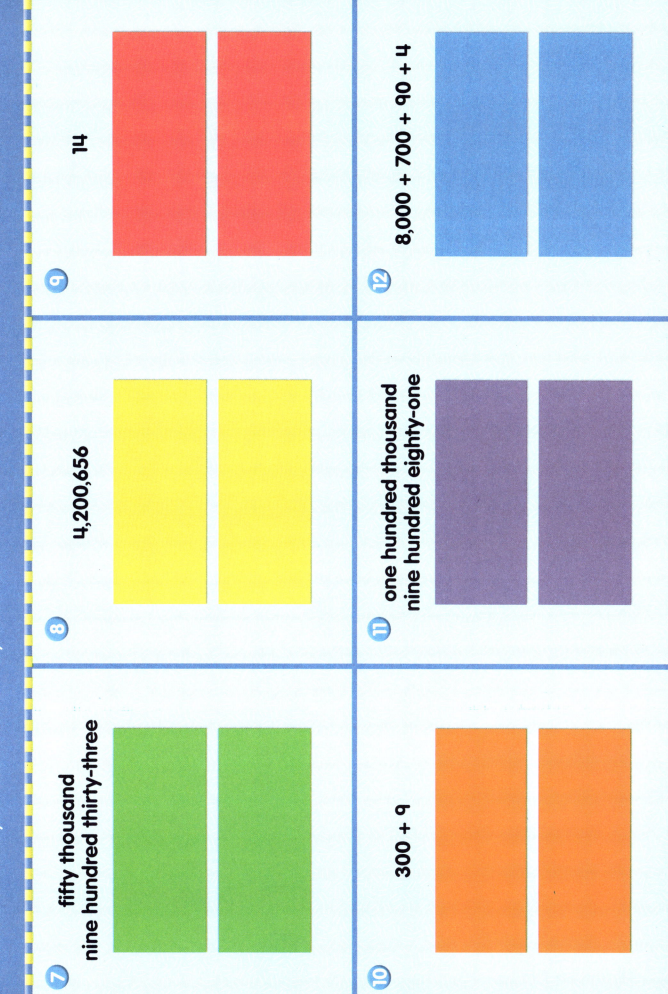

8. 4,200,656

9. 14

10. 300 + 9

11. one hundred thousand
nine hundred eighty-one

12. 8,000 + 700 + 90 + 4

twenty-seven	eighty-five	one hundred seventy-four	365
one thousand seven hundred forty-two	nine thousand eight hundred twenty	50,933	four million two hundred thousand six hundred fifty-six
fourteen	three hundred nine	100,981	eight thousand seven hundred ninety-four
20 + 7	85	100 + 70 + 4	300 + 60 + 5
1,000 + 700 + 40 + 2	9,820	50,000 + 900 + 30 + 3	4,000,000 + 200,000 + 600 + 50 + 6
10 + 4	309	100,000 + 900 + 80 + 1	8,794

Numbers, Numbers, Numbers! EMC 3074 © Evan-Moor Corp.	Numbers, Numbers, Numbers! EMC 3074 © Evan-Moor Corp.	Numbers, Numbers, Numbers! EMC 3074 © Evan-Moor Corp.	Numbers, Numbers, Numbers! EMC 3074 © Evan-Moor Corp.
Numbers, Numbers, Numbers! EMC 3074 © Evan-Moor Corp.	Numbers, Numbers, Numbers! EMC 3074 © Evan-Moor Corp.	Numbers, Numbers, Numbers! EMC 3074 © Evan-Moor Corp.	Numbers, Numbers, Numbers! EMC 3074 © Evan-Moor Corp.
Numbers, Numbers, Numbers! EMC 3074 © Evan-Moor Corp.	Numbers, Numbers, Numbers! EMC 3074 © Evan-Moor Corp.	Numbers, Numbers, Numbers! EMC 3074 © Evan-Moor Corp.	Numbers, Numbers, Numbers! EMC 3074 © Evan-Moor Corp.
Numbers, Numbers, Numbers! EMC 3074 © Evan-Moor Corp.	Numbers, Numbers, Numbers! EMC 3074 © Evan-Moor Corp.	Numbers, Numbers, Numbers! EMC 3074 © Evan-Moor Corp.	Numbers, Numbers, Numbers! EMC 3074 © Evan-Moor Corp.
Numbers, Numbers, Numbers! EMC 3074 © Evan-Moor Corp.	Numbers, Numbers, Numbers! EMC 3074 © Evan-Moor Corp.	Numbers, Numbers, Numbers! EMC 3074 © Evan-Moor Corp.	Numbers, Numbers, Numbers! EMC 3074 © Evan-Moor Corp.
Numbers, Numbers, Numbers! EMC 3074 © Evan-Moor Corp.	Numbers, Numbers, Numbers! EMC 3074 © Evan-Moor Corp.	Numbers, Numbers, Numbers! EMC 3074 © Evan-Moor Corp.	Numbers, Numbers, Numbers! EMC 3074 © Evan-Moor Corp.

Take It to Your Seat Centers

Rounding Big Numbers

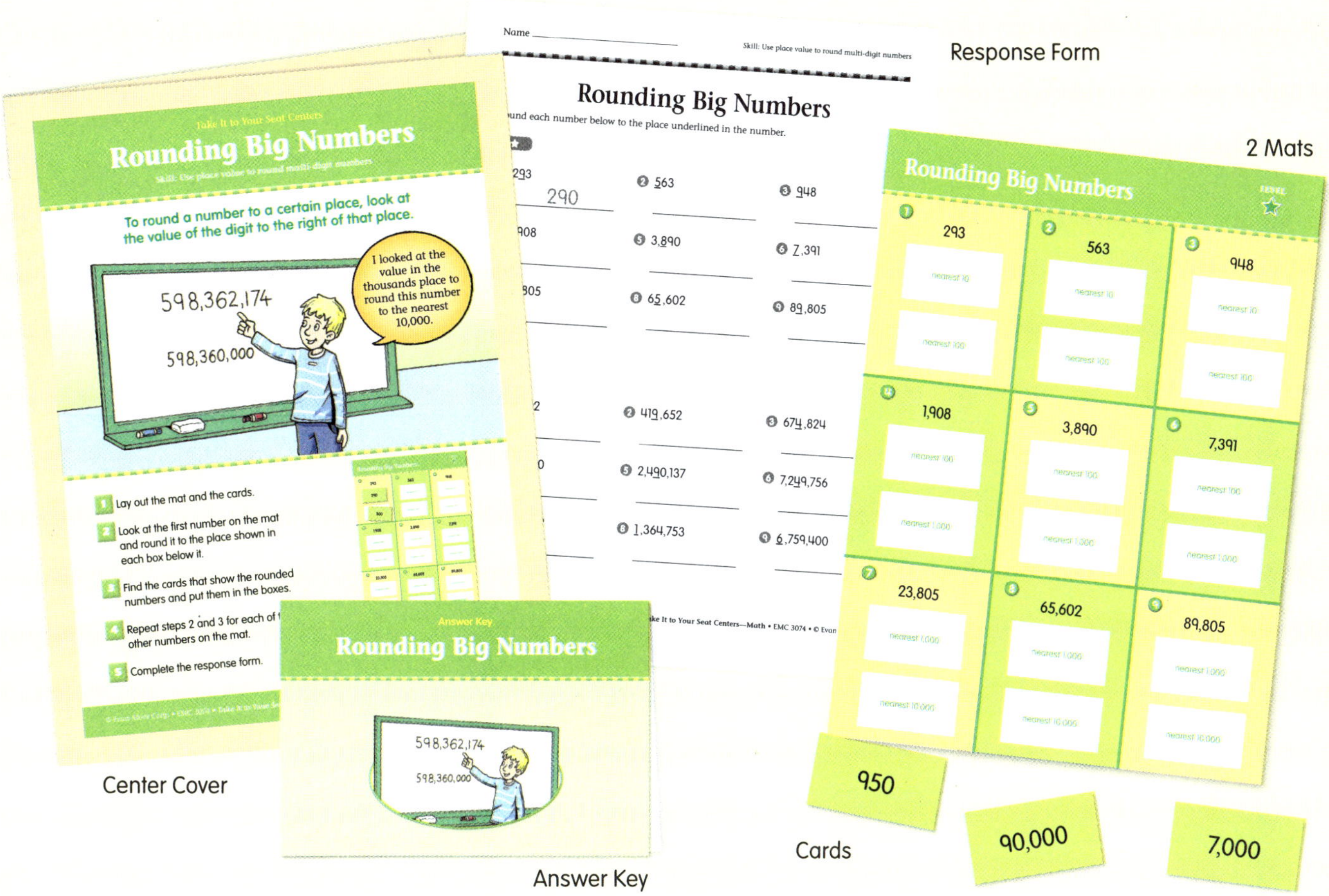

Skill: Use place value to round multi-digit numbers

Steps to Follow

1. **Prepare the center.** (See page 3.)
2. **Introduce the center.** State the goal. Say: *You will round 3- to 7-digit numbers to a specific place, from the nearest ten to the nearest million.*
3. **Teach the skill.** Demonstrate how to use the center with individual students or small groups.
4. **Practice the skill.** Have students use the center independently or with a partner.

Contents

Name ______________________ Skill: Use place value to round multi-digit numbers

Rounding Big Numbers

Round each number below to the place underlined in the number.

★

1. 293
   290
2. 563
3. 948
4. 1,908
5. 3,890
6. 7,391
7. 23,805
8. 65,602
9. 89,805

★★

1. 508,902
2. 419,652
3. 674,824
4. 1,806,900
5. 2,490,137
6. 7,249,756
7. 4,870,652
8. 1,364,753
9. 6,759,400

Take It to Your Seat Centers

Rounding Big Numbers

Skill: Use place value to round multi-digit numbers

To round a number to a certain place, look at the value of the digit to the right of that place.

598,362,174
598,360,000
I looked at the value in the thousands place to round this number to the nearest 10,000.

1. Lay out the mat and the cards.
2. Look at the first number on the mat and round it to the place shown in each box below it.
3. Find the cards that show the rounded numbers and put them in the boxes.
4. Repeat steps 2 and 3 for each of the other numbers on the mat.
5. Complete the response form.

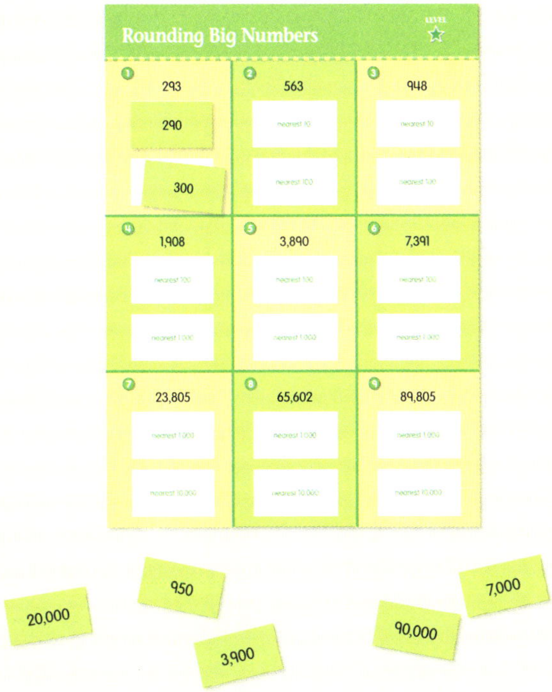

Rounding Big Numbers

Answer Key

(fold)

Response Form

Rounding Big Numbers

Round each number below to the place underlined in the number.

★

1. 293 — 290	2. 563 — 600	3. 948 — 900
4. 1,908 — 2,000	5. 3,890 — 3,900	6. 7,391 — 7,000
7. 23,805 — 20,000	8. 65,602 — 66,000	9. 89,805 — 90,000

★★

1. 508,902 — 510,000	2. 419,652 — 420,000	3. 674,824 — 675,000
4. 1,806,900 — 1,800,000	5. 2,490,137 — 2,490,000	6. 7,249,756 — 7,250,000
7. 4,870,652 — 4,871,000	8. 1,364,753 — 1,000,000	9. 6,759,400 — 7,000,000

Answer Key

Rounding Big Numbers

Rounding Big Numbers — LEVEL ☆

1. 293	2. 563	3. 948
290	560	950
300	600	900
4. 1,908	5. 3,890	6. 7,391
1,900	3,900	7,400
2,000	4,000	7,000
7. 23,805	8. 65,602	9. 89,805
24,000	66,000	90,000
20,000	70,000	90,000

Rounding Big Numbers — LEVEL ☆☆

1. 508,902	2. 419,652	3. 674,824
509,000	420,000	675,000
510,000	420,000	700,000
4. 1,806,900	5. 2,490,137	6. 7,249,756
1,807,000	2,490,000	7,250,000
1,800,000	2,500,000	7,200,000
7. 4,870,652	8. 1,364,753	9. 6,759,400
4,871,000	1,360,000	6,800,000
5,000,000	1,000,000	7,000,000

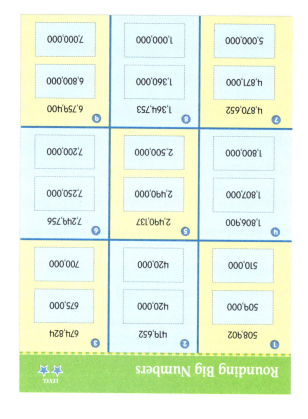

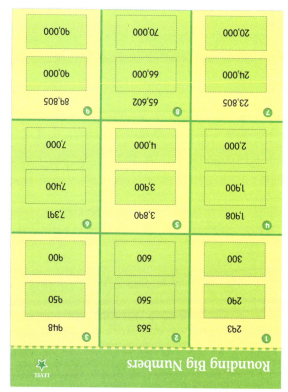

Rounding Big Numbers

LEVEL ☆

1. 293
   - nearest 10
   - nearest 100

2. 563
   - nearest 10
   - nearest 100

3. 948
   - nearest 10
   - nearest 100

4. 1,908
   - nearest 100
   - nearest 1,000

5. 3,890
   - nearest 100
   - nearest 1,000

6. 7,391
   - nearest 100
   - nearest 1,000

7. 23,805
   - nearest 1,000
   - nearest 10,000

8. 65,602
   - nearest 1,000
   - nearest 10,000

9. 89,805
   - nearest 1,000
   - nearest 10,000

Rounding Big Numbers

LEVEL ★★

1. 508,902	2. 419,652	3. 674,824
nearest 1,000	nearest 1,000	nearest 1,000
nearest 10,000	nearest 10,000	nearest 100,000
4. 1,806,900	5. 2,490,137	6. 7,249,756
nearest 1,000	nearest 10,000	nearest 10,000
nearest 100,000	nearest 100,000	nearest 100,000
7. 4,870,652	8. 1,364,753	9. 6,759,400
nearest 1,000	nearest 10,000	nearest 100,000
nearest 1,000,000	nearest 1,000,000	nearest 1,000,000

290	300	560	600
950	900	1,900	2,000
3,900	4,000	7,400	7,000
24,000	20,000	90,000	90,000
66,000	70,000	1,807,000	1,800,000
420,000	420,000	675,000	700,000
2,490,000	2,500,000	509,000	510,000
7,250,000	7,200,000	4,871,000	5,000,000
1,360,000	1,000,000	6,800,000	7,000,000

Rounding Big Numbers
EMC 3074
© Evan-Moor Corp.

Rounding Big Numbers
EMC 3074
© Evan-Moor Corp.

Rounding Big Numbers
EMC 3074
© Evan-Moor Corp.

Rounding Big Numbers
EMC 3074
© Evan-Moor Corp.

Rounding Big Numbers
EMC 3074
© Evan-Moor Corp.

Rounding Big Numbers
EMC 3074
© Evan-Moor Corp.

Rounding Big Numbers
EMC 3074
© Evan-Moor Corp.

Rounding Big Numbers
EMC 3074
© Evan-Moor Corp.

Rounding Big Numbers
EMC 3074
© Evan-Moor Corp.

Rounding Big Numbers
EMC 3074
© Evan-Moor Corp.

Rounding Big Numbers
EMC 3074
© Evan-Moor Corp.

Rounding Big Numbers
EMC 3074
© Evan-Moor Corp.

Rounding Big Numbers
EMC 3074
© Evan-Moor Corp.

Rounding Big Numbers
EMC 3074
© Evan-Moor Corp.

Rounding Big Numbers
EMC 3074
© Evan-Moor Corp.

Rounding Big Numbers
EMC 3074
© Evan-Moor Corp.

Rounding Big Numbers
EMC 3074
© Evan-Moor Corp.

Rounding Big Numbers
EMC 3074
© Evan-Moor Corp.

Rounding Big Numbers
EMC 3074
© Evan-Moor Corp.

Rounding Big Numbers
EMC 3074
© Evan-Moor Corp.

Rounding Big Numbers
EMC 3074
© Evan-Moor Corp.

Rounding Big Numbers
EMC 3074
© Evan-Moor Corp.

Rounding Big Numbers
EMC 3074
© Evan-Moor Corp.

Rounding Big Numbers
EMC 3074
© Evan-Moor Corp.

Rounding Big Numbers
EMC 3074
© Evan-Moor Corp.

Rounding Big Numbers
EMC 3074
© Evan-Moor Corp.

Rounding Big Numbers
EMC 3074
© Evan-Moor Corp.

Rounding Big Numbers
EMC 3074
© Evan-Moor Corp.

Rounding Big Numbers
EMC 3074
© Evan-Moor Corp.

Rounding Big Numbers
EMC 3074
© Evan-Moor Corp.

Rounding Big Numbers
EMC 3074
© Evan-Moor Corp.

Rounding Big Numbers
EMC 3074
© Evan-Moor Corp.

Rounding Big Numbers
EMC 3074
© Evan-Moor Corp.

Rounding Big Numbers
EMC 3074
© Evan-Moor Corp.

Rounding Big Numbers
EMC 3074
© Evan-Moor Corp.

Rounding Big Numbers
EMC 3074
© Evan-Moor Corp.

Take It to Your Seat Centers

Equivalent Fractions

Skill: Identify equivalent fractions based on visual models

Steps to Follow

1. **Prepare the center.** (See page 3.)
2. **Introduce the center.** State the goal. Say: *You will match pairs of equivalent fractions using models as guides.*
3. **Teach the skill.** Demonstrate how to use the center with individual students or small groups.
4. **Practice the skill.** Have students use the center independently or with a partner.

Contents

Equivalent Fractions

Look at the mats. Complete each blank shape below to show the equivalent fraction. Then write the equivalent fraction after the equal sign.

1. 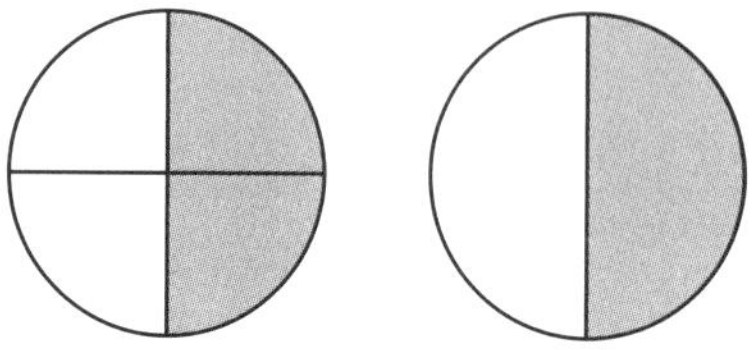
$\frac{2}{4} = \frac{1}{2}$

2. 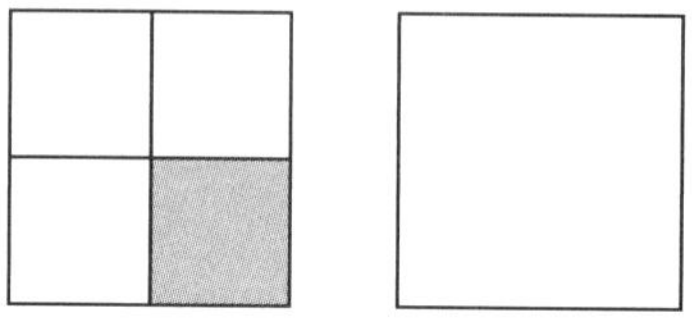
$\frac{1}{4} =$ ______

3. 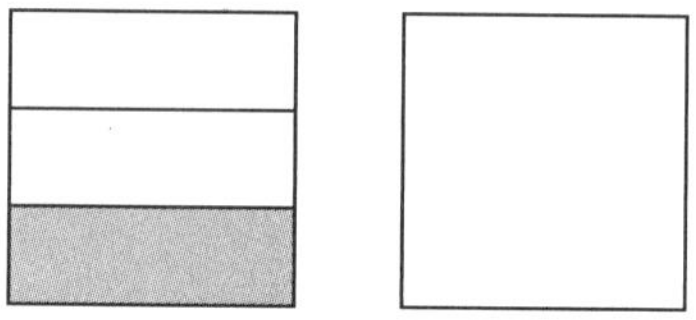
$\frac{1}{3} =$ ______

4. 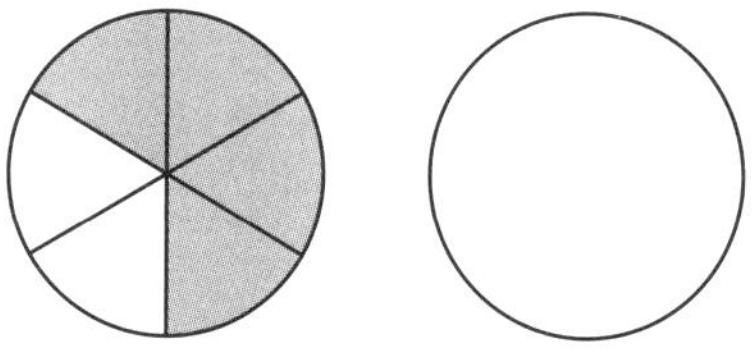
$\frac{4}{6} =$ ______

5. 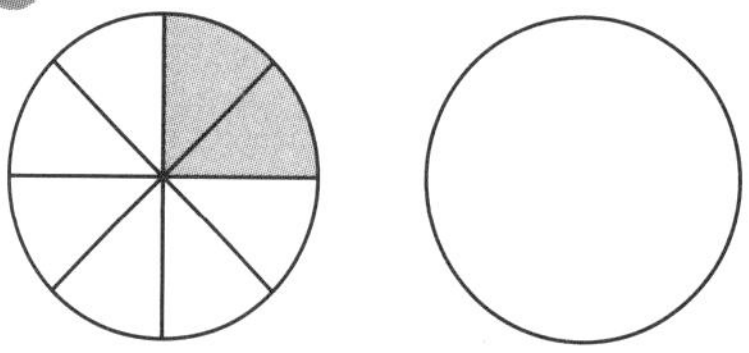
$\frac{2}{8} =$ ______

6. 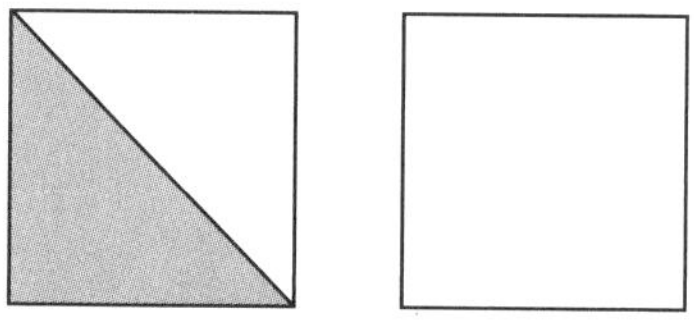
$\frac{1}{2} =$ ______

7. 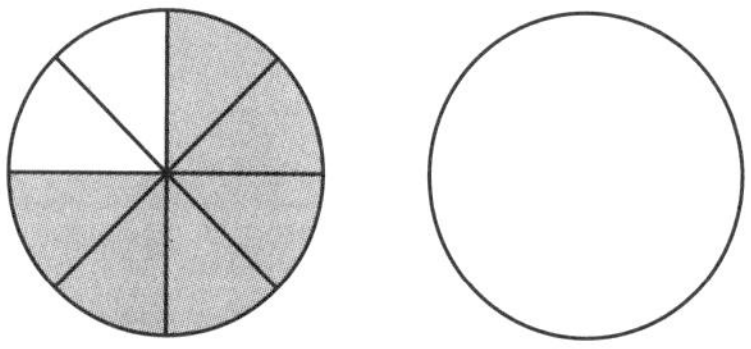
$\frac{6}{8} =$ ______

8. 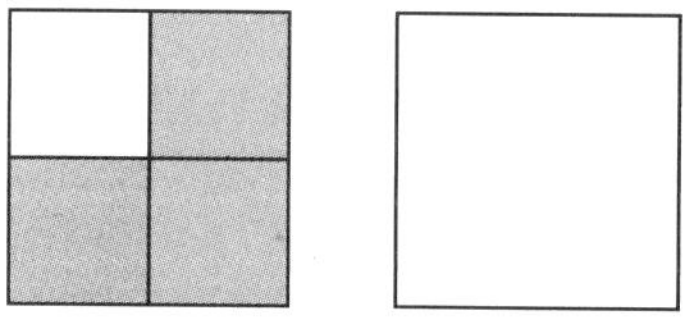
$\frac{3}{4} =$ ______

9. 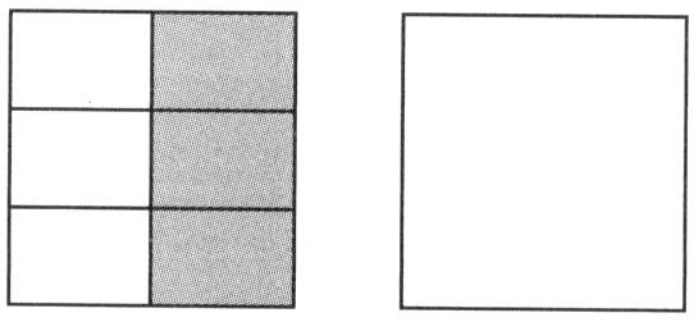
$\frac{3}{6} =$ ______

10. 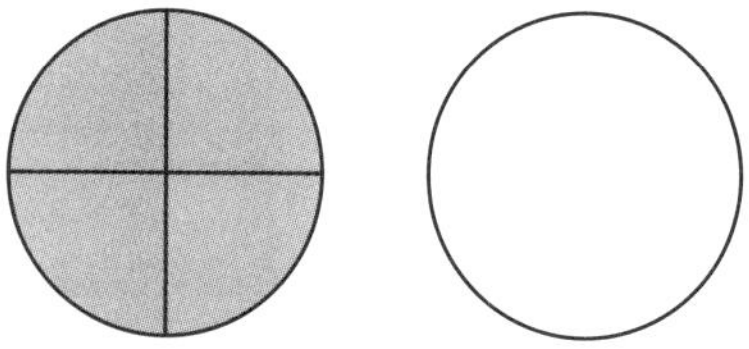
$\frac{4}{4} =$ ______

11. 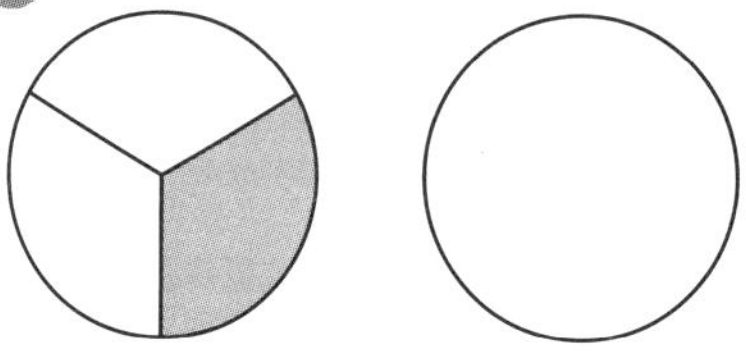
$\frac{1}{3} =$ ______

12. 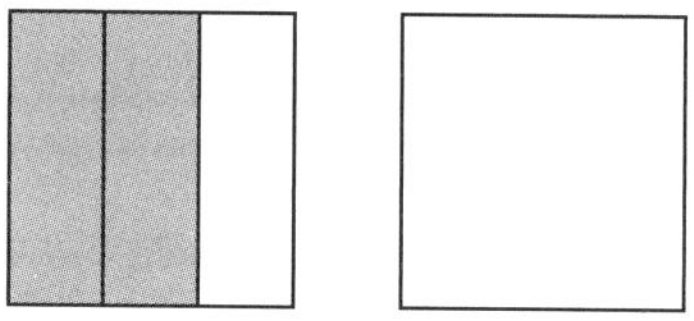
$\frac{2}{3} =$ ______

Equivalent Fractions

Skill: Identify equivalent fractions

Different fractions can name the same amount.

$$\frac{1}{2} = \frac{2}{4}$$

Half of your sandwich is the same amount as two-fourths of mine.

1. Lay out the mats and sort the cards into two groups: fractions and models.
2. Match each fraction card with a model card that shows the fraction.
3. Look at each model and fraction on the mats and find the model and fraction cards that are equivalent.
4. Place the cards in the labeled boxes.
5. Complete the response form.

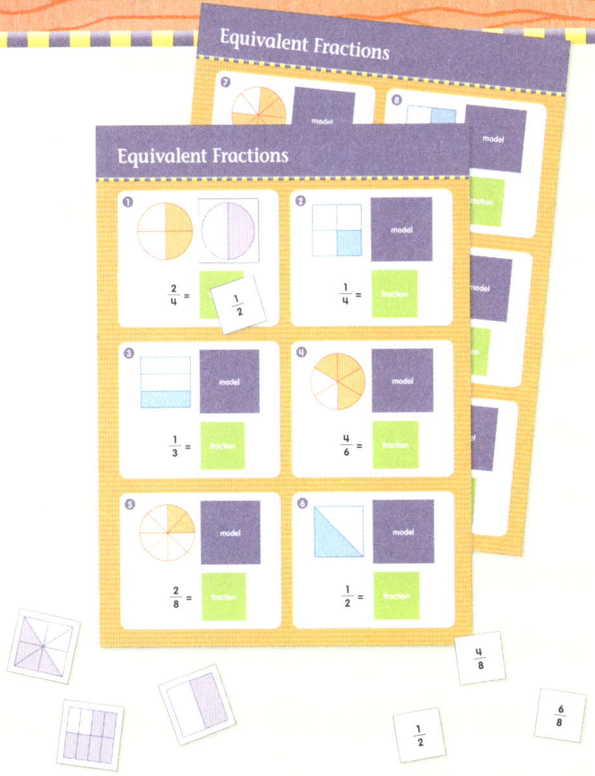

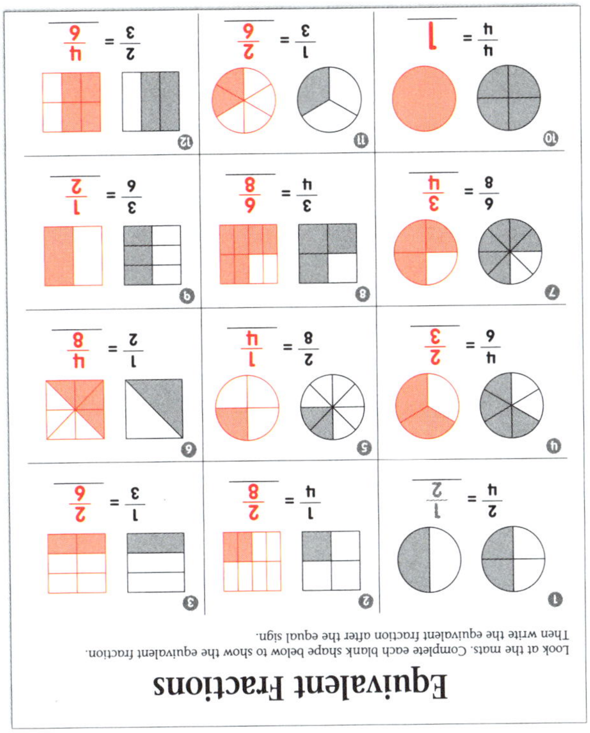

Response Form

(fold)

Answer Key

Equivalent Fractions

Answer Key

Equivalent Fractions

Equivalent Fractions

1. 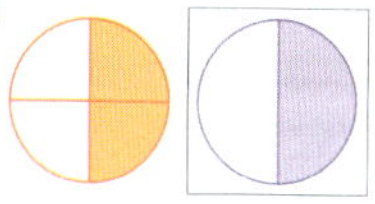

$\frac{2}{4} = \frac{1}{2}$

2. 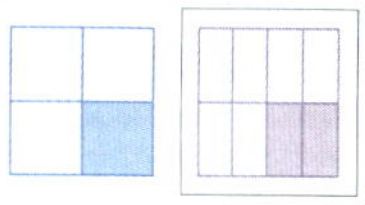

$\frac{1}{4} = \frac{2}{8}$

3. 

$\frac{1}{3} = \frac{2}{6}$

4. 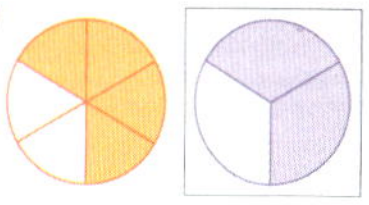

$\frac{4}{6} = \frac{2}{3}$

5. 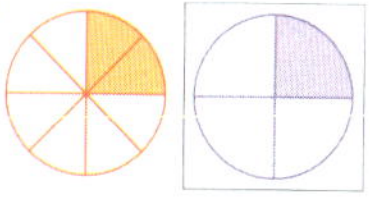

$\frac{2}{8} = \frac{1}{4}$

6. 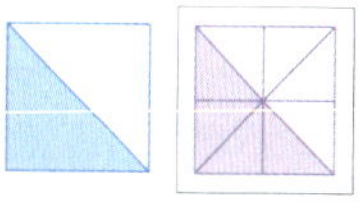

$\frac{1}{2} = \frac{4}{8}$

Equivalent Fractions

7. 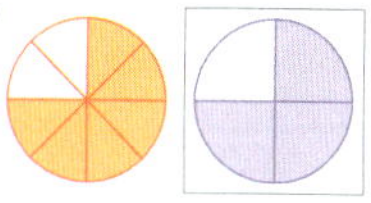

$\frac{6}{8} = \frac{3}{4}$

8. 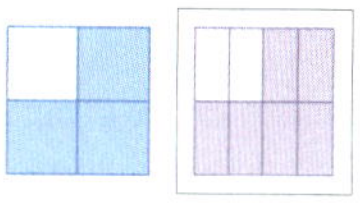

$\frac{3}{4} = \frac{6}{8}$

9. 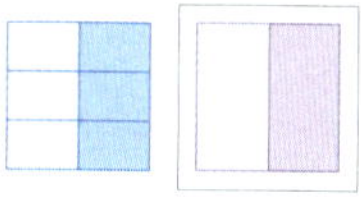

$\frac{3}{6} = \frac{1}{2}$

10. 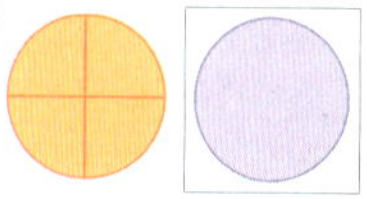

$\frac{4}{4} = 1$

11. 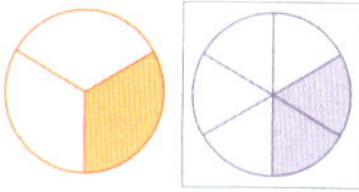

$\frac{1}{3} = \frac{2}{6}$

12. 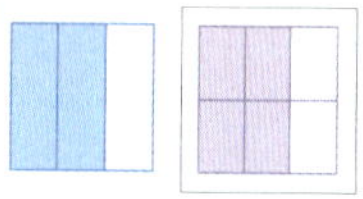

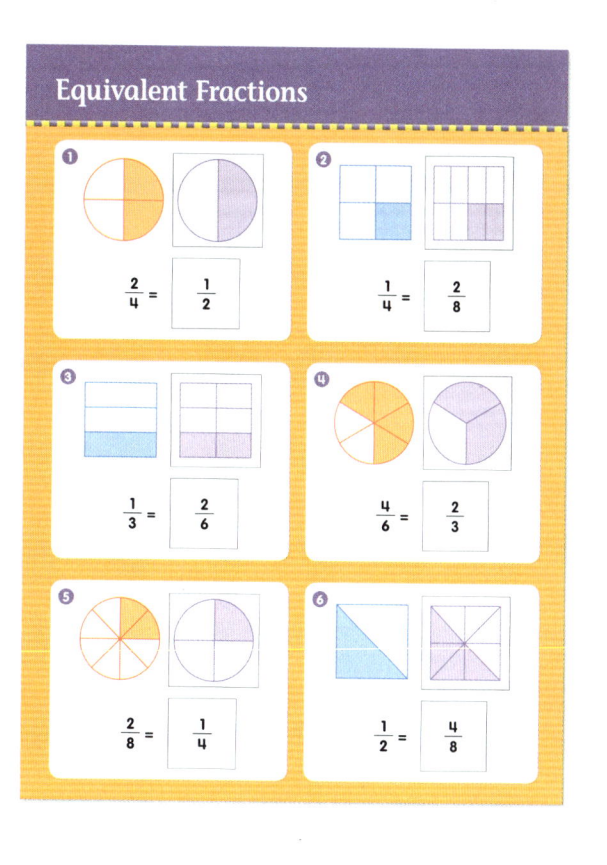

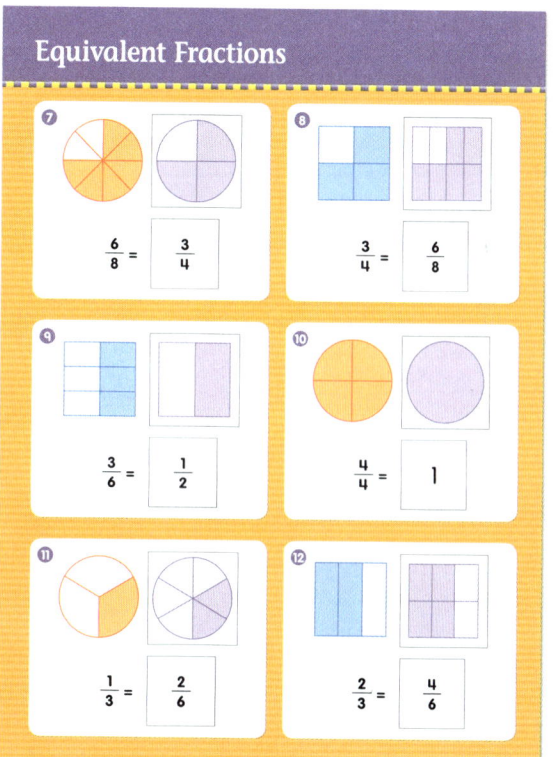

$\frac{2}{3} = \frac{4}{6}$

Equivalent Fractions

1

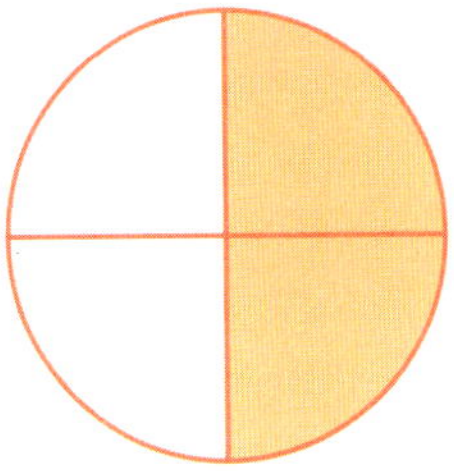

model

$\frac{2}{4} =$ fraction

2

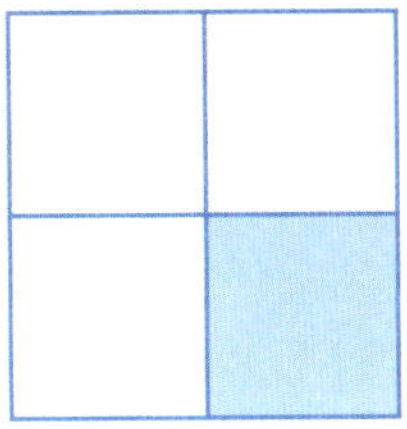

model

$\frac{1}{4} =$ fraction

3

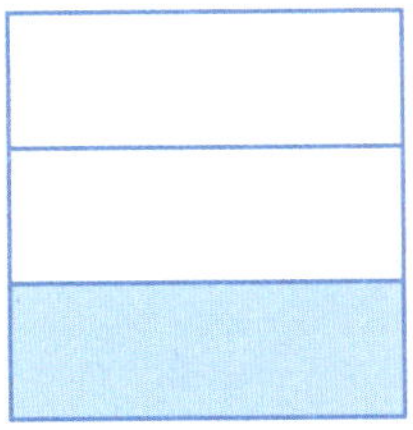

model

$\frac{1}{3} =$ fraction

4

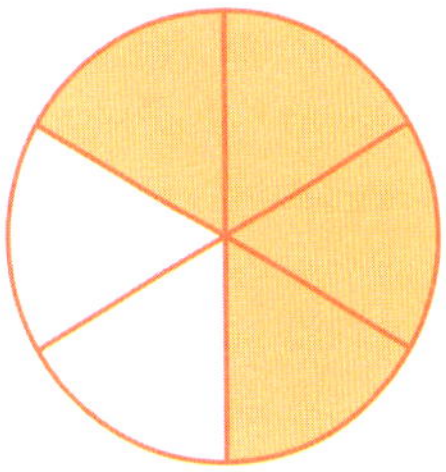

model

$\frac{4}{6} =$ fraction

5

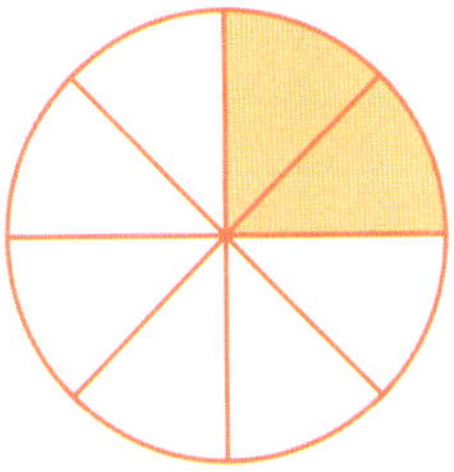

model

$\frac{2}{8} =$ fraction

6

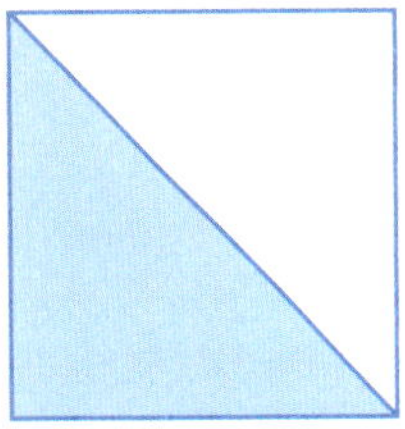

model

$\frac{1}{2} =$ fraction

Equivalent Fractions

7

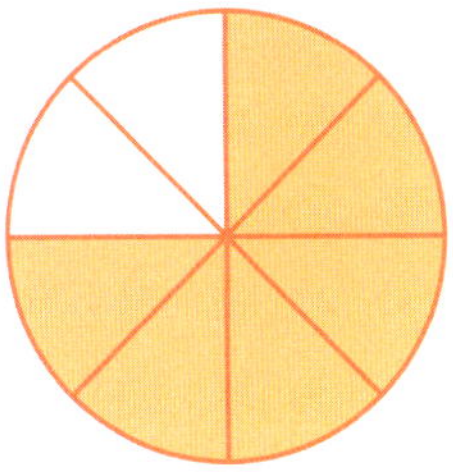

model

$\frac{6}{8} =$ fraction

8

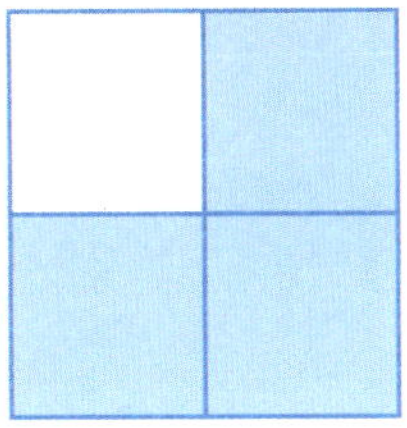

model

$\frac{3}{4} =$ fraction

9

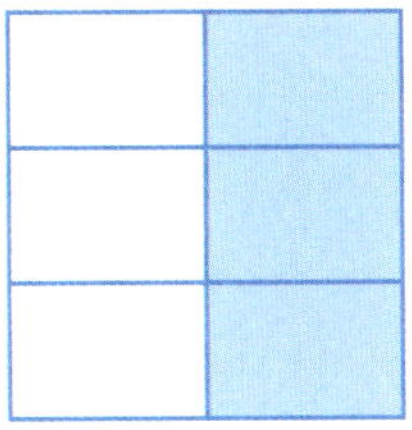

model

$\frac{3}{6} =$ fraction

10

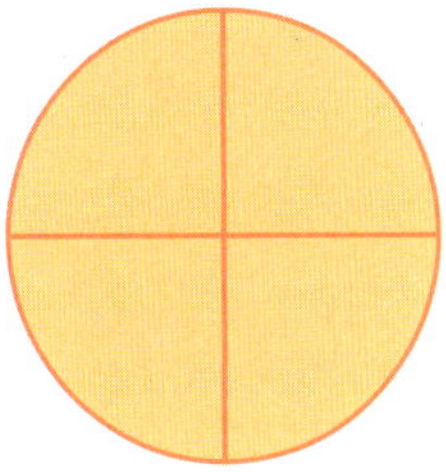

model

$\frac{4}{4} =$ fraction

11

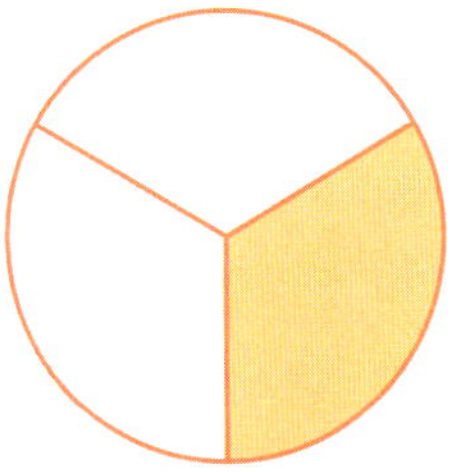

model

$\frac{1}{3} =$ fraction

12

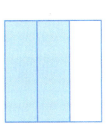

model

$\frac{2}{3} =$ fraction

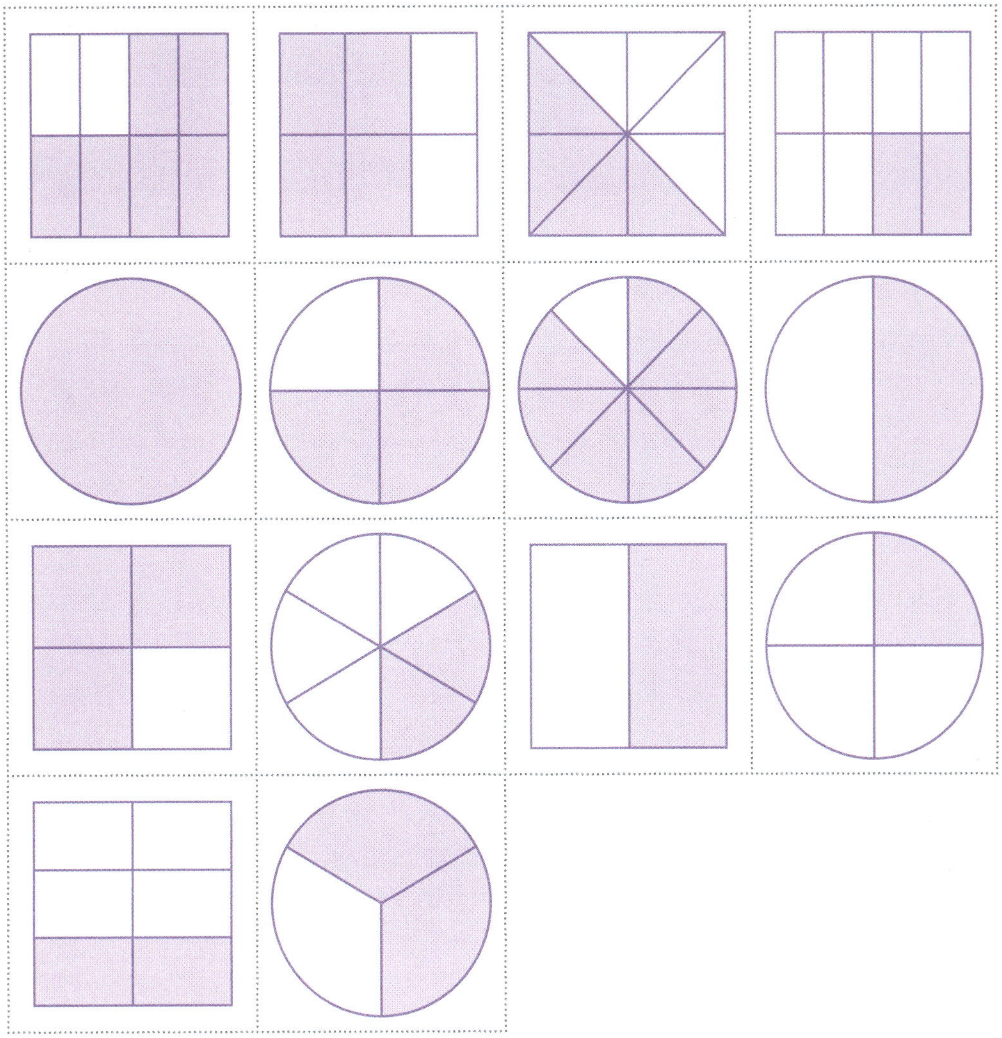

$\frac{6}{8}$	$\frac{3}{4}$	$\frac{1}{2}$	$\frac{2}{8}$	$\frac{3}{4}$	$\frac{2}{6}$	$\frac{2}{3}$
1	$\frac{4}{6}$	$\frac{2}{6}$	$\frac{1}{2}$	$\frac{7}{8}$	$\frac{4}{8}$	$\frac{1}{4}$

Equivalent Fractions
EMC 3074
© Evan-Moor Corp.

Equivalent Fractions
EMC 3074
© Evan-Moor Corp.

Equivalent Fractions
EMC 3074
© Evan-Moor Corp.

Equivalent Fractions
EMC 3074
© Evan-Moor Corp.

Equivalent Fractions
EMC 3074
© Evan-Moor Corp.

Equivalent Fractions
EMC 3074
© Evan-Moor Corp.

Equivalent Fractions
EMC 3074
© Evan-Moor Corp.

Equivalent Fractions
EMC 3074
© Evan-Moor Corp.

Equivalent Fractions
EMC 3074
© Evan-Moor Corp.

Equivalent Fractions
EMC 3074
© Evan-Moor Corp.

Equivalent Fractions
EMC 3074
© Evan-Moor Corp.

Equivalent Fractions
EMC 3074
© Evan-Moor Corp.

Equivalent Fractions
EMC 3074
© Evan-Moor Corp.

Equivalent Fractions
EMC 3074
© Evan-Moor Corp.

Equivalent Fractions
EMC 3074
© Evan-Moor Corp.

Equivalent Fractions
EMC 3074
© Evan-Moor Corp.

Equivalent Fractions
EMC 3074
© Evan-Moor Corp.

Equivalent Fractions
EMC 3074
© Evan-Moor Corp.

Equivalent Fractions
EMC 3074
© Evan-Moor Corp.

Equivalent Fractions
EMC 3074
© Evan-Moor Corp.

Equivalent Fractions
EMC 3074
© Evan-Moor Corp.

Equivalent Fractions
EMC 3074
© Evan-Moor Corp.

Equivalent Fractions
EMC 3074
© Evan-Moor Corp.

Equivalent Fractions
EMC 3074
© Evan-Moor Corp.

Equivalent Fractions
EMC 3074
© Evan-Moor Corp.

Equivalent Fractions
EMC 3074
© Evan-Moor Corp.

Equivalent Fractions
EMC 3074
© Evan-Moor Corp.

Take It to Your Seat Centers

Relative Values of Fractions

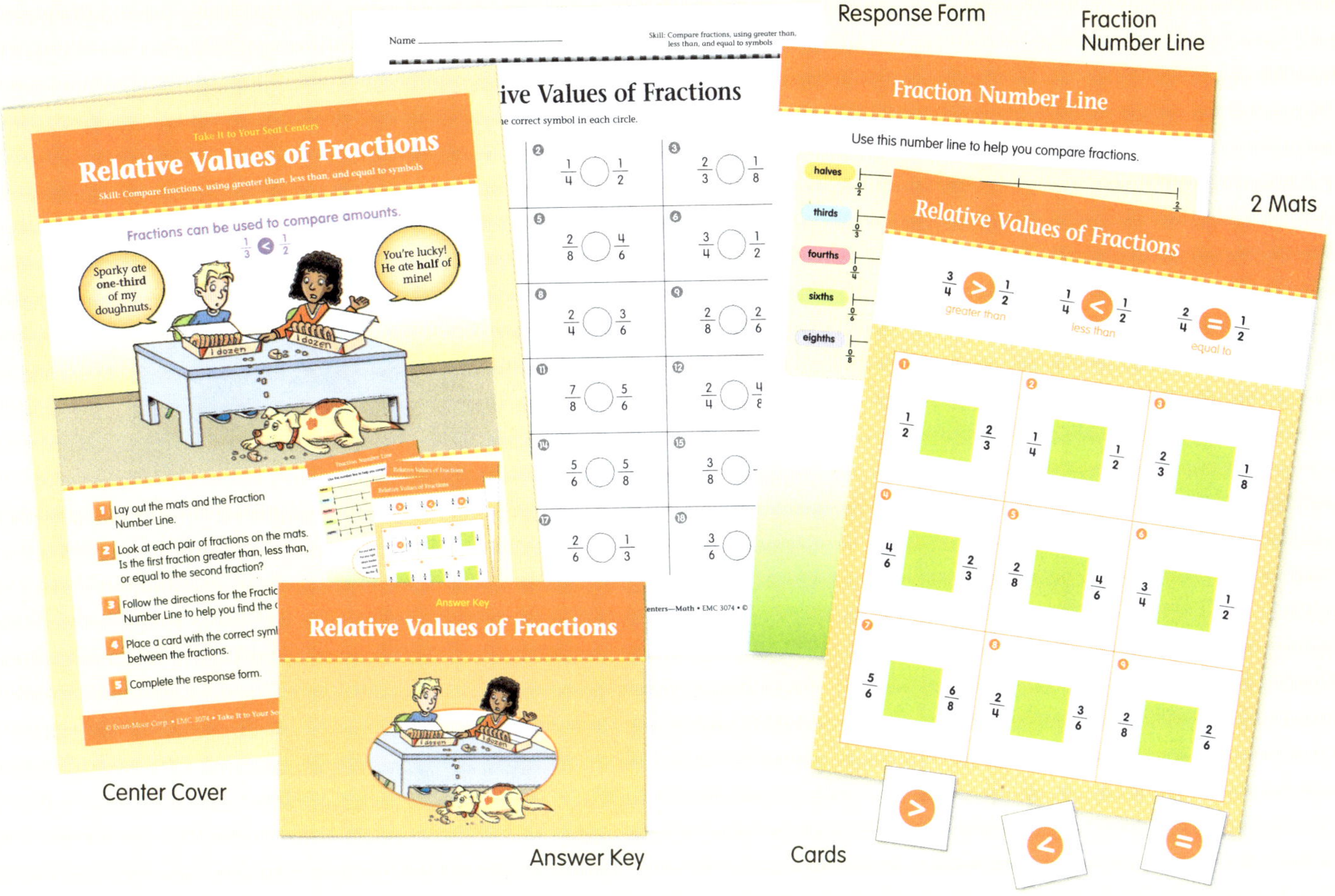

Skill: Compare fractions, using greater than, less than, and equal to symbols

Steps to Follow

1. **Prepare the center.** (See page 3.)
2. **Introduce the center.** State the goal. Say: *You will use a fraction number line to help you compare values of fractions that have different denominators.*
3. **Teach the skill.** Demonstrate how to use the center with individual students or small groups.
4. **Practice the skill.** Have students use the center independently or with a partner.

Contents

Name ______________________________

Skill: Compare fractions, using greater than, less than, and equal to symbols

Relative Values of Fractions

Look at the mats. Draw the correct symbol in each circle.

1. $\frac{1}{2}$ ◯ $\frac{2}{3}$	2. $\frac{1}{4}$ ◯ $\frac{1}{2}$	3. $\frac{2}{3}$ ◯ $\frac{1}{8}$
4. $\frac{4}{6}$ ◯ $\frac{2}{3}$	5. $\frac{2}{8}$ ◯ $\frac{4}{6}$	6. $\frac{3}{4}$ ◯ $\frac{1}{2}$
7. $\frac{5}{6}$ ◯ $\frac{6}{8}$	8. $\frac{2}{4}$ ◯ $\frac{3}{6}$	9. $\frac{2}{8}$ ◯ $\frac{2}{6}$
10. $\frac{3}{4}$ ◯ $\frac{5}{8}$	11. $\frac{7}{8}$ ◯ $\frac{5}{6}$	12. $\frac{2}{4}$ ◯ $\frac{4}{8}$
13. $\frac{4}{6}$ ◯ $\frac{3}{4}$	14. $\frac{5}{6}$ ◯ $\frac{5}{8}$	15. $\frac{3}{8}$ ◯ $\frac{1}{3}$
16. $\frac{1}{8}$ ◯ $\frac{1}{6}$	17. $\frac{2}{6}$ ◯ $\frac{1}{3}$	18. $\frac{3}{6}$ ◯ $\frac{3}{8}$

Relative Values of Fractions

Skill: Compare fractions, using greater than, less than, and equal to symbols

Fractions can be used to compare amounts.

$\frac{1}{3} < \frac{1}{2}$

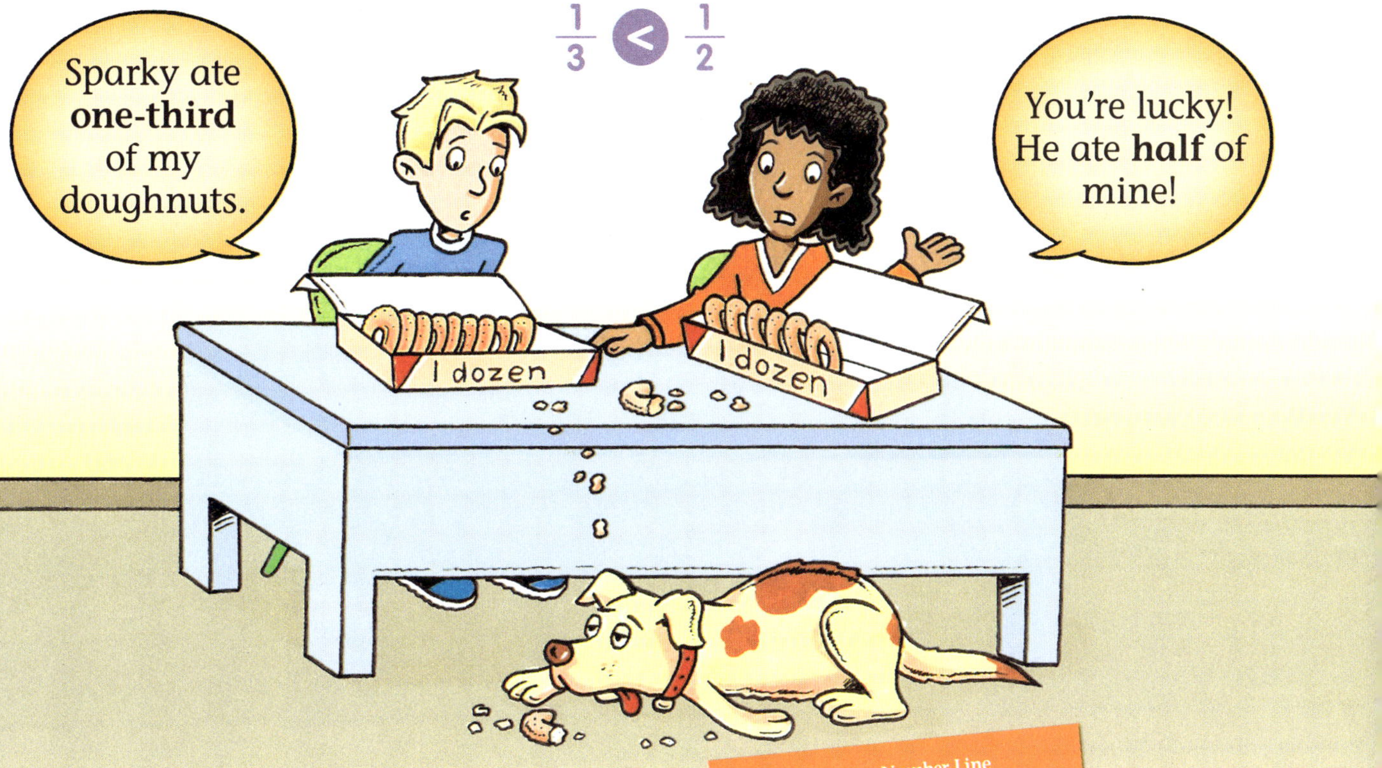

Sparky ate **one-third** of my doughnuts.
You're lucky! He ate **half** of mine!
1 dozen
1 dozen

1. Lay out the mats and the Fraction Number Line.
2. Look at each pair of fractions on the mats. Is the first fraction greater than, less than, or equal to the second fraction?
3. Follow the directions for the Fraction Number Line to help you find the answer.
4. Place a card with the correct symbol between the fractions.
5. Complete the response form.

Answer Key

Relative Values of Fractions

(fold)

Response Form

Relative Values of Fractions

Look at the mats. Draw the correct symbol in each circle.

1. $\frac{1}{2} < \frac{2}{3}$	2. $\frac{1}{4} < \frac{1}{2}$	3. $\frac{2}{3} > \frac{1}{8}$
4. $\frac{4}{6} = \frac{2}{3}$	5. $\frac{2}{8} < \frac{4}{6}$	6. $\frac{3}{4} > \frac{1}{2}$
7. $\frac{5}{6} > \frac{6}{8}$	8. $\frac{2}{4} = \frac{3}{6}$	9. $\frac{2}{8} < \frac{2}{6}$
10. $\frac{3}{4} > \frac{5}{8}$	11. $\frac{7}{8} > \frac{5}{6}$	12. $\frac{2}{4} = \frac{4}{8}$
13. $\frac{4}{6} < \frac{3}{4}$	14. $\frac{5}{6} > \frac{5}{8}$	15. $\frac{3}{8} > \frac{1}{3}$
16. $\frac{1}{8} < \frac{1}{6}$	17. $\frac{2}{6} = \frac{1}{3}$	18. $\frac{3}{6} > \frac{3}{8}$

Answer Key

Relative Values of Fractions

Relative Values of Fractions

$\frac{3}{4} > \frac{1}{2}$ greater than

$\frac{1}{4} < \frac{1}{2}$ less than

$\frac{2}{4} = \frac{1}{2}$ equal to

1 $\frac{1}{2} < \frac{2}{3}$	2 $\frac{1}{4} < \frac{1}{2}$	3 $\frac{2}{3} > \frac{1}{8}$
4 $\frac{4}{6} = \frac{2}{3}$	5 $\frac{2}{8} < \frac{4}{6}$	6 $\frac{3}{4} > \frac{1}{2}$
7 $\frac{5}{6} > \frac{6}{8}$	8 $\frac{2}{4} = \frac{3}{6}$	9 $\frac{2}{8} < \frac{2}{6}$

Relative Values of Fractions

$\frac{3}{4} > \frac{1}{2}$ greater than

$\frac{1}{4} < \frac{1}{2}$ less than

$\frac{2}{4} = \frac{1}{2}$ equal to

10 $\frac{3}{4} > \frac{5}{8}$	11 $\frac{7}{8} > \frac{5}{6}$	12 $\frac{2}{4} = \frac{4}{8}$
13 $\frac{4}{6} < \frac{3}{4}$	14 $\frac{5}{6} > \frac{5}{8}$	15 $\frac{3}{8} > \frac{1}{3}$
16 $\frac{1}{8} < \frac{1}{6}$	17 $\frac{2}{6} = \frac{1}{3}$	18 $\frac{3}{6} > \frac{3}{8}$

Fraction Number Line

Use this number line to help you compare fractions.

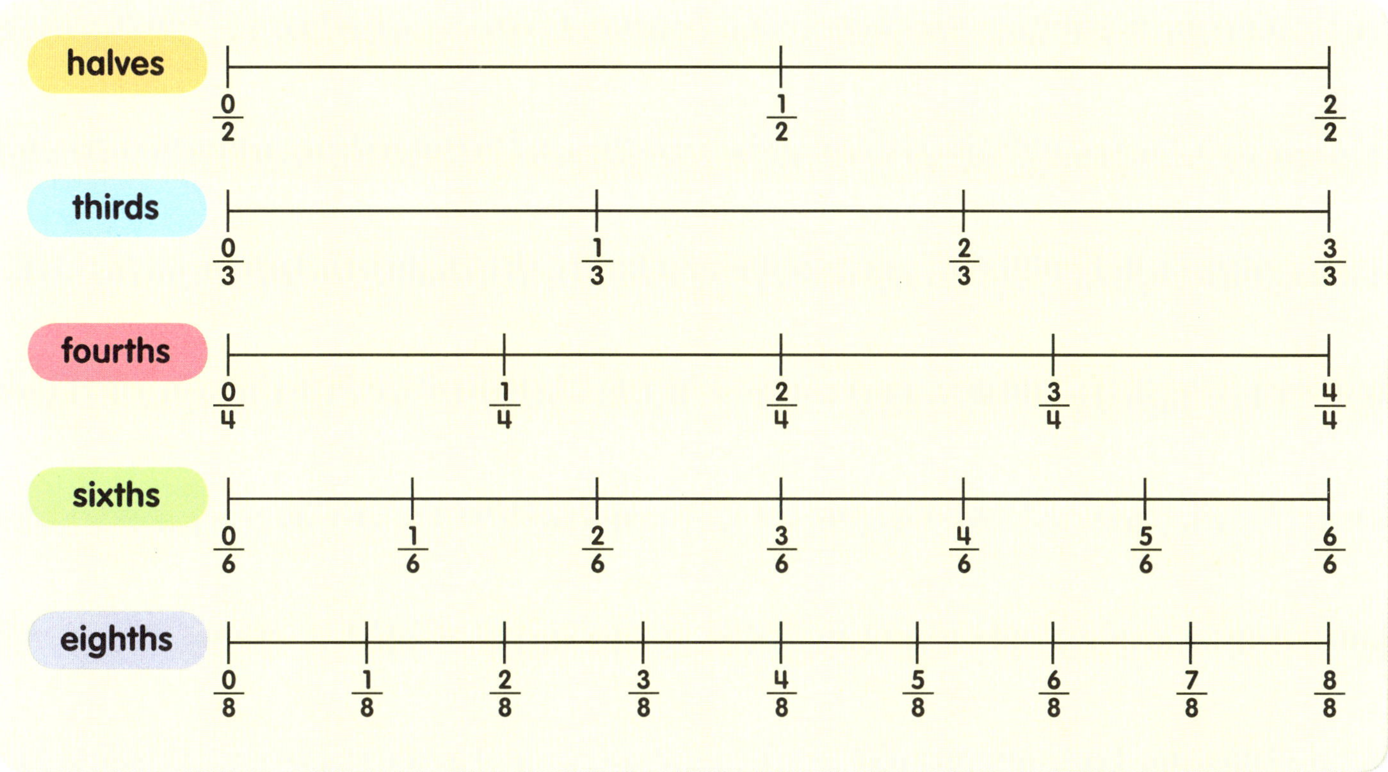

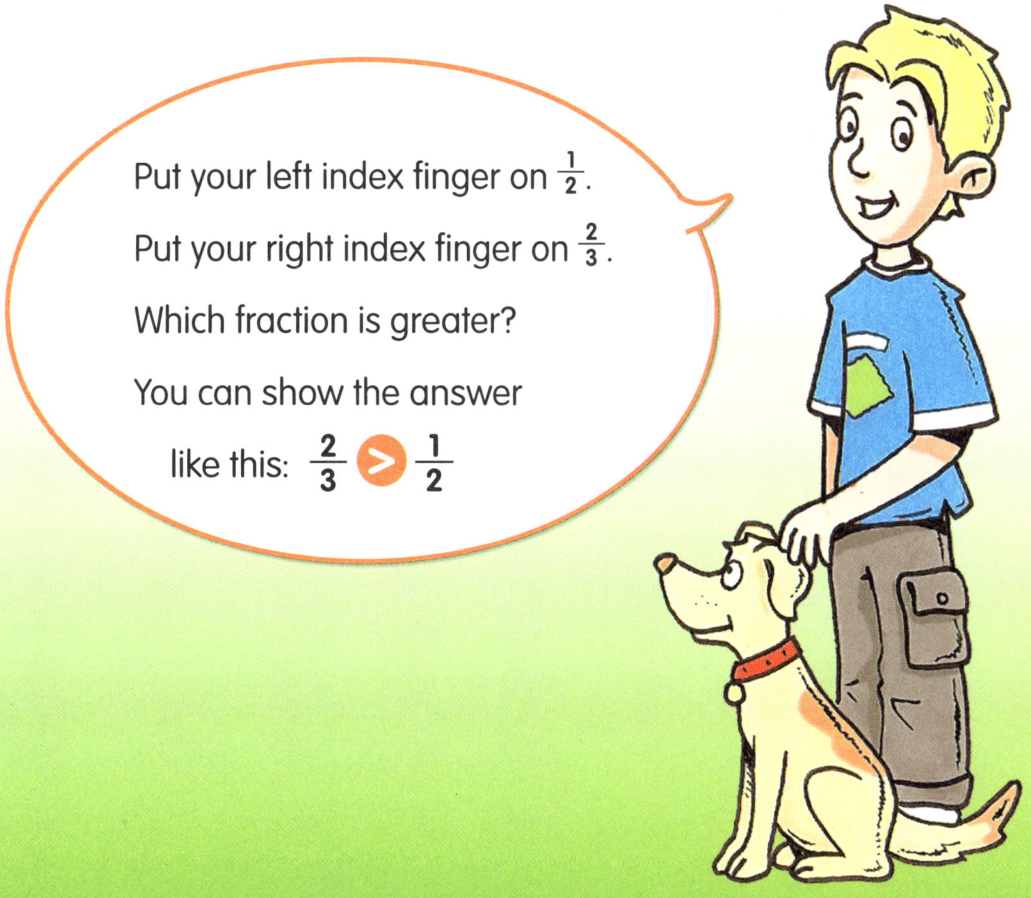

Put your left index finger on $\frac{1}{2}$.
Put your right index finger on $\frac{2}{3}$.
Which fraction is greater?
You can show the answer
like this: $\frac{2}{3} > \frac{1}{2}$

Relative Values of Fractions

$\frac{3}{4} > \frac{1}{2}$ greater than

$\frac{1}{4} < \frac{1}{2}$ less than

$\frac{2}{4} = \frac{1}{2}$ equal to

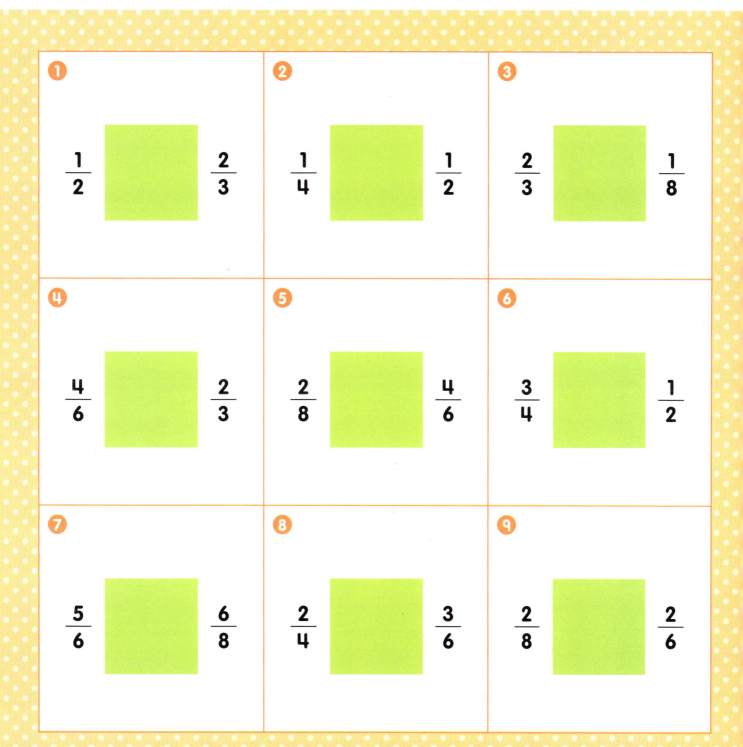

1. $\frac{1}{2}$ ☐ $\frac{2}{3}$
2. $\frac{1}{4}$ ☐ $\frac{1}{2}$
3. $\frac{2}{3}$ ☐ $\frac{1}{8}$
4. $\frac{4}{6}$ ☐ $\frac{2}{3}$
5. $\frac{2}{8}$ ☐ $\frac{4}{6}$
6. $\frac{3}{4}$ ☐ $\frac{1}{2}$
7. $\frac{5}{6}$ ☐ $\frac{6}{8}$
8. $\frac{2}{4}$ ☐ $\frac{3}{6}$
9. $\frac{2}{8}$ ☐ $\frac{2}{6}$

Relative Values of Fractions

$\frac{3}{4} > \frac{1}{2}$ greater than

$\frac{1}{4} < \frac{1}{2}$ less than

$\frac{2}{4} = \frac{1}{2}$ equal to

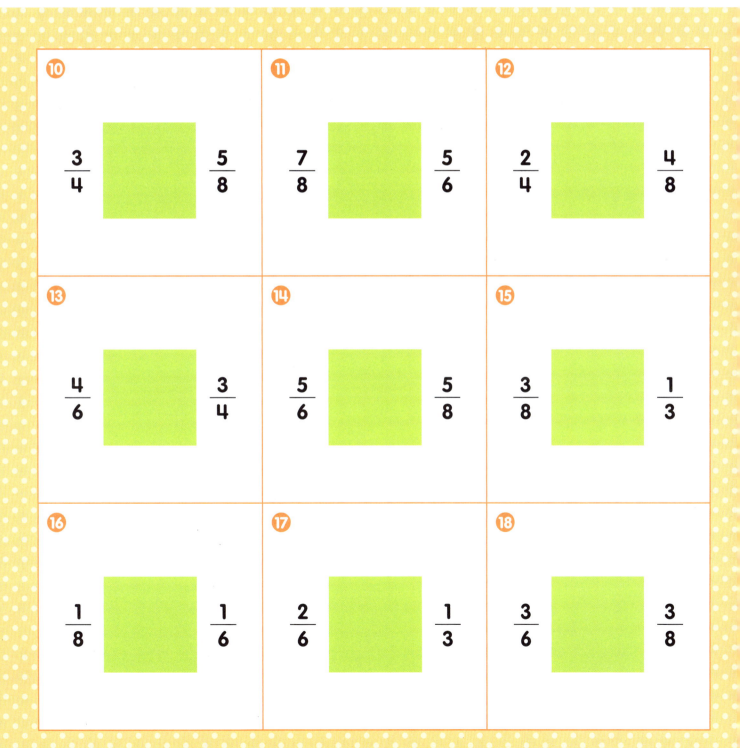

10. $\frac{3}{4}$ ☐ $\frac{5}{8}$

11. $\frac{7}{8}$ ☐ $\frac{5}{6}$

12. $\frac{2}{4}$ ☐ $\frac{4}{8}$

13. $\frac{4}{6}$ ☐ $\frac{3}{4}$

14. $\frac{5}{6}$ ☐ $\frac{5}{8}$

15. $\frac{3}{8}$ ☐ $\frac{1}{3}$

16. $\frac{1}{8}$ ☐ $\frac{1}{6}$

17. $\frac{2}{6}$ ☐ $\frac{1}{3}$

18. $\frac{3}{6}$ ☐ $\frac{3}{8}$

>	>	>	>	>	>	>
>	>	>	>	>	>	>
>	>	>	>	>	>	>
<	<	<	<	<	<	<
<	<	<	<	<	<	<
<	<	<	<	<	<	<
=	=	=	=	=	=	=
=	=	=	=	=	=	=
=	=	=	=	=	=	=

Relative Values of Fractions EMC 3074 © Evan-Moor Corp.	Relative Values of Fractions EMC 3074 © Evan-Moor Corp.	Relative Values of Fractions EMC 3074 © Evan-Moor Corp.	Relative Values of Fractions EMC 3074 © Evan-Moor Corp.	Relative Values of Fractions EMC 3074 © Evan-Moor Corp.	Relative Values of Fractions EMC 3074 © Evan-Moor Corp.	Relative Values of Fractions EMC 3074 © Evan-Moor Corp.
Relative Values of Fractions EMC 3074 © Evan-Moor Corp.	Relative Values of Fractions EMC 3074 © Evan-Moor Corp.	Relative Values of Fractions EMC 3074 © Evan-Moor Corp.	Relative Values of Fractions EMC 3074 © Evan-Moor Corp.	Relative Values of Fractions EMC 3074 © Evan-Moor Corp.	Relative Values of Fractions EMC 3074 © Evan-Moor Corp.	Relative Values of Fractions EMC 3074 © Evan-Moor Corp.
Relative Values of Fractions EMC 3074 © Evan-Moor Corp.	Relative Values of Fractions EMC 3074 © Evan-Moor Corp.	Relative Values of Fractions EMC 3074 © Evan-Moor Corp.	Relative Values of Fractions EMC 3074 © Evan-Moor Corp.	Relative Values of Fractions EMC 3074 © Evan-Moor Corp.	Relative Values of Fractions EMC 3074 © Evan-Moor Corp.	Relative Values of Fractions EMC 3074 © Evan-Moor Corp.
Relative Values of Fractions EMC 3074 © Evan-Moor Corp.	Relative Values of Fractions EMC 3074 © Evan-Moor Corp.	Relative Values of Fractions EMC 3074 © Evan-Moor Corp.	Relative Values of Fractions EMC 3074 © Evan-Moor Corp.	Relative Values of Fractions EMC 3074 © Evan-Moor Corp.	Relative Values of Fractions EMC 3074 © Evan-Moor Corp.	Relative Values of Fractions EMC 3074 © Evan-Moor Corp.
Relative Values of Fractions EMC 3074 © Evan-Moor Corp.	Relative Values of Fractions EMC 3074 © Evan-Moor Corp.	Relative Values of Fractions EMC 3074 © Evan-Moor Corp.	Relative Values of Fractions EMC 3074 © Evan-Moor Corp.	Relative Values of Fractions EMC 3074 © Evan-Moor Corp.	Relative Values of Fractions EMC 3074 © Evan-Moor Corp.	Relative Values of Fractions EMC 3074 © Evan-Moor Corp.
Relative Values of Fractions EMC 3074 © Evan-Moor Corp.	Relative Values of Fractions EMC 3074 © Evan-Moor Corp.	Relative Values of Fractions EMC 3074 © Evan-Moor Corp.	Relative Values of Fractions EMC 3074 © Evan-Moor Corp.	Relative Values of Fractions EMC 3074 © Evan-Moor Corp.	Relative Values of Fractions EMC 3074 © Evan-Moor Corp.	Relative Values of Fractions EMC 3074 © Evan-Moor Corp.
Relative Values of Fractions EMC 3074 © Evan-Moor Corp.	Relative Values of Fractions EMC 3074 © Evan-Moor Corp.	Relative Values of Fractions EMC 3074 © Evan-Moor Corp.	Relative Values of Fractions EMC 3074 © Evan-Moor Corp.	Relative Values of Fractions EMC 3074 © Evan-Moor Corp.	Relative Values of Fractions EMC 3074 © Evan-Moor Corp.	Relative Values of Fractions EMC 3074 © Evan-Moor Corp.
Relative Values of Fractions EMC 3074 © Evan-Moor Corp.	Relative Values of Fractions EMC 3074 © Evan-Moor Corp.	Relative Values of Fractions EMC 3074 © Evan-Moor Corp.	Relative Values of Fractions EMC 3074 © Evan-Moor Corp.	Relative Values of Fractions EMC 3074 © Evan-Moor Corp.	Relative Values of Fractions EMC 3074 © Evan-Moor Corp.	Relative Values of Fractions EMC 3074 © Evan-Moor Corp.
Relative Values of Fractions EMC 3074 © Evan-Moor Corp.	Relative Values of Fractions EMC 3074 © Evan-Moor Corp.	Relative Values of Fractions EMC 3074 © Evan-Moor Corp.	Relative Values of Fractions EMC 3074 © Evan-Moor Corp.	Relative Values of Fractions EMC 3074 © Evan-Moor Corp.	Relative Values of Fractions EMC 3074 © Evan-Moor Corp.	Relative Values of Fractions EMC 3074 © Evan-Moor Corp.

Take It to Your Seat Centers

Decimal Fractions

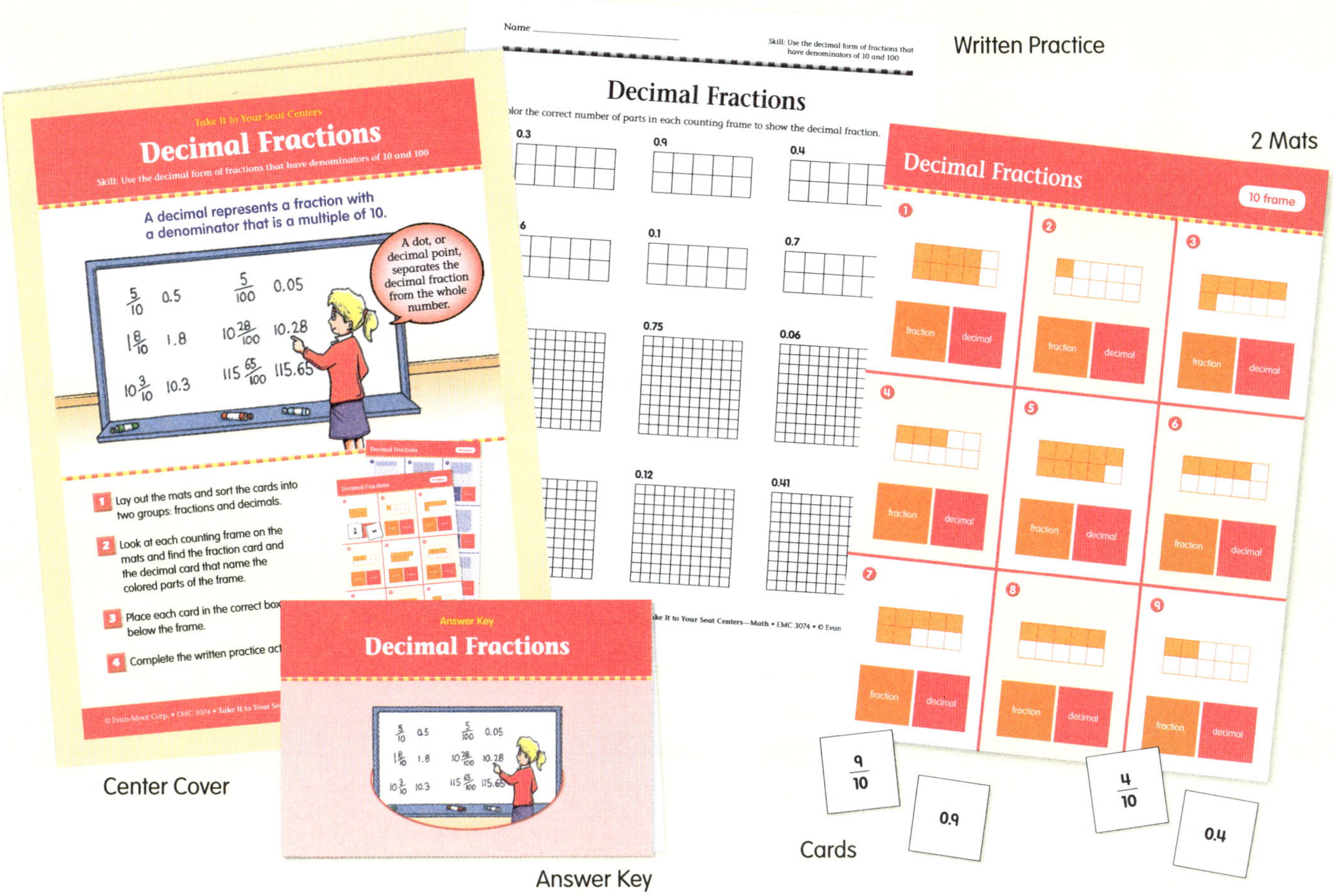

Written Practice
2 Mats
Center Cover
Answer Key
Cards
Decimal Fractions
A decimal represents a fraction with a denominator that is a multiple of 10.
A dot, or decimal point, separates the decimal fraction from the whole number.
Lay out the mats and sort the cards into two groups: fractions and decimals.
Look at each counting frame on the mats and find the fraction card and the decimal card that name the colored parts of the frame.
Answer Key
Decimal Fractions
10 frame
fraction
decimal
0.9
0.4

Skill: Use the decimal form of fractions that have denominators of 10 and 100

Steps to Follow

1. **Prepare the center.** (See page 3.)
2. **Introduce the center.** State the goal. Say: *You will find cards that show the fraction and the decimal form for each counting frame on the mats.*
3. **Teach the skill.** Demonstrate how to use the center with individual students or small groups.
4. **Practice the skill.** Have students use the center independently or with a partner.

Contents

Name ______________________

Skill: Use the decimal form of fractions that have denominators of 10 and 100

Decimal Fractions

Color the correct number of parts in each counting frame to show the decimal fraction.

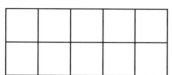

0.3

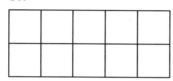

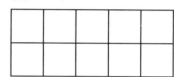

0.9

0.4

0.6

0.1

0.7

0.33

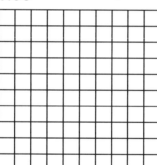

0.75

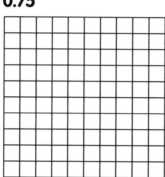

0.06

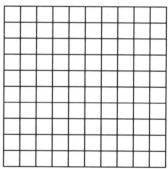

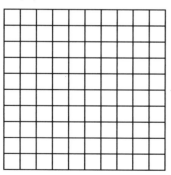

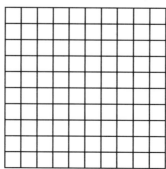

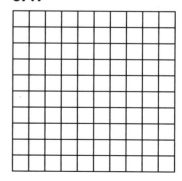

0.89

0.12

0.41

Take It to Your Seat Centers

Decimal Fractions

Skill: Use the decimal form of fractions that have denominators of 10 and 100

A decimal represents a fraction with a denominator that is a multiple of 10.

1. Lay out the mats and sort the cards into two groups: fractions and decimals.
2. Look at each counting frame on the mats and find the fraction card and the decimal card that name the colored parts of the frame.
3. Place each card in the correct box below the frame.
4. Complete the written practice activity.

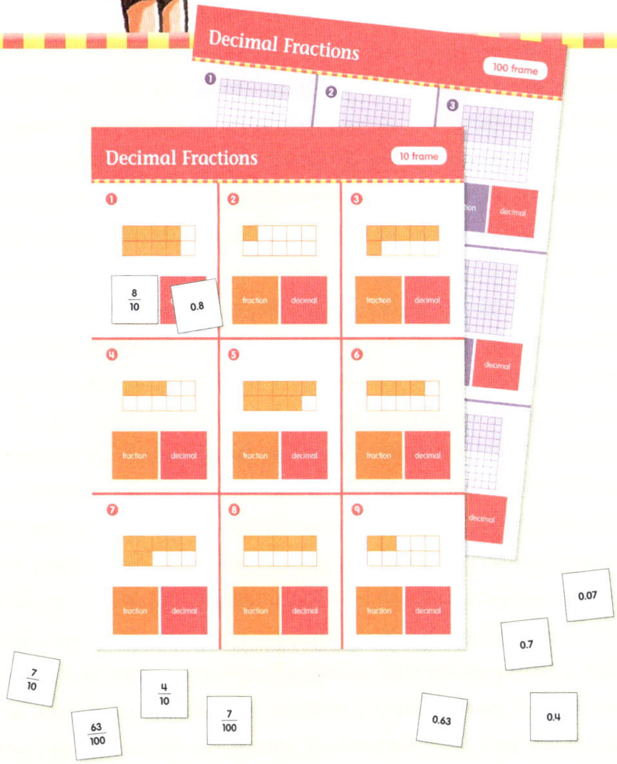

Written Practice

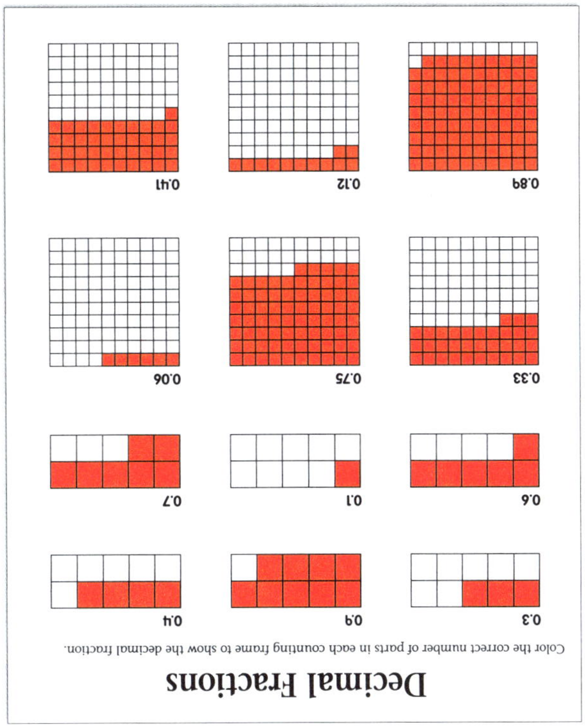

(fold)

Answer Key

Decimal Fractions

Answer Key

Decimal Fractions

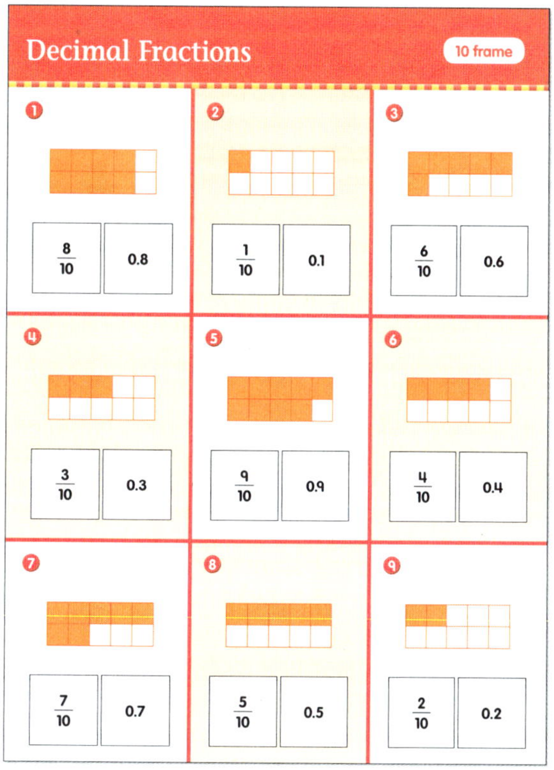

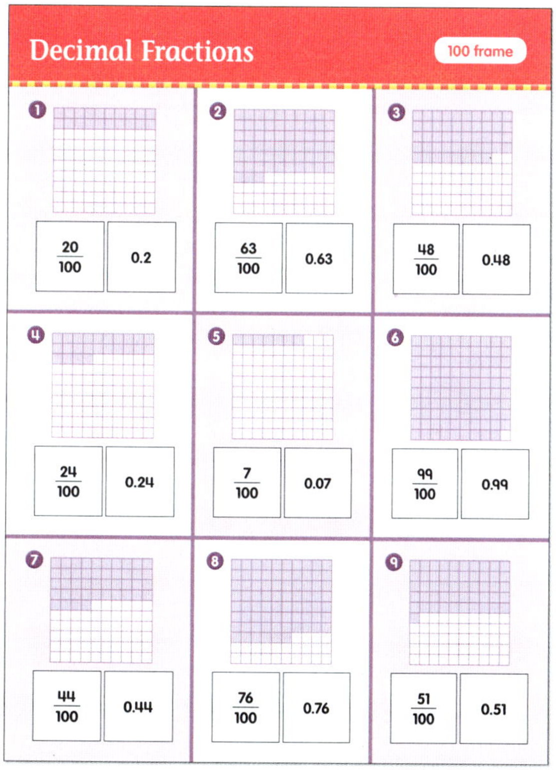

Decimal Fractions

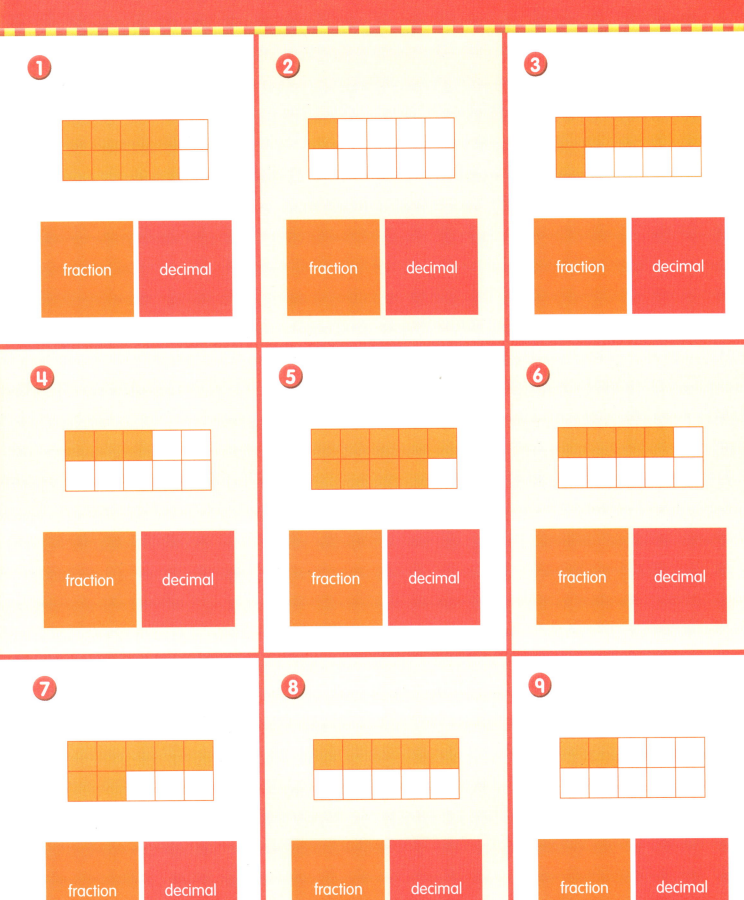

10 frame

1

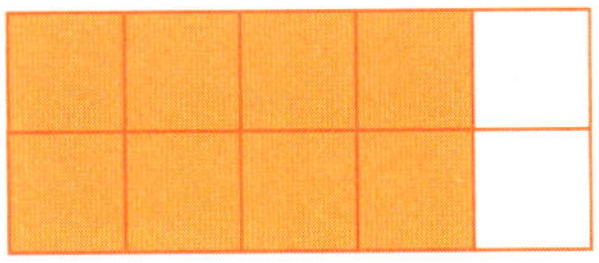

fraction

decimal

2

fraction

decimal

3

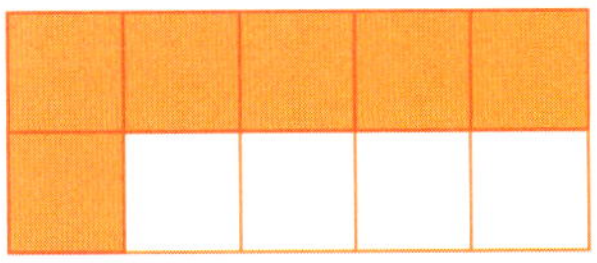

fraction

decimal

4

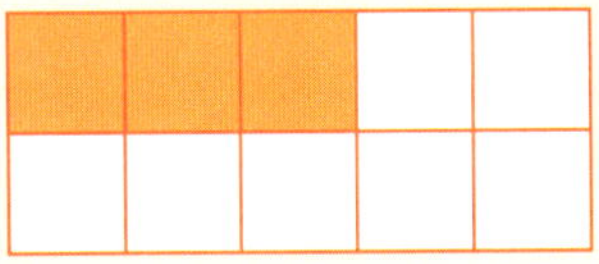

fraction

decimal

5

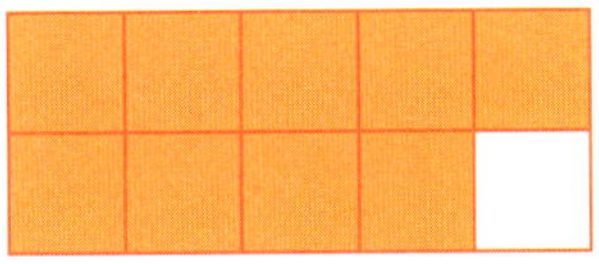

fraction

decimal

6

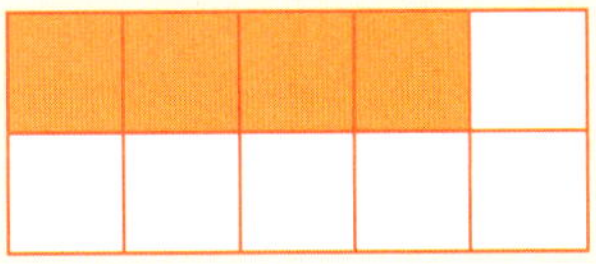

fraction

decimal

7

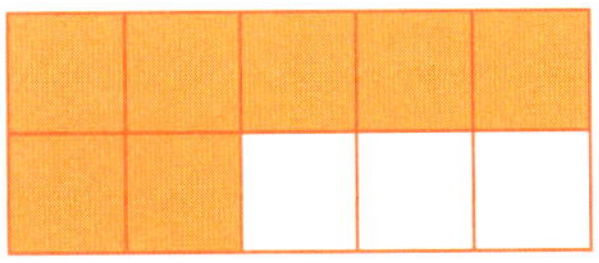

fraction

decimal

8

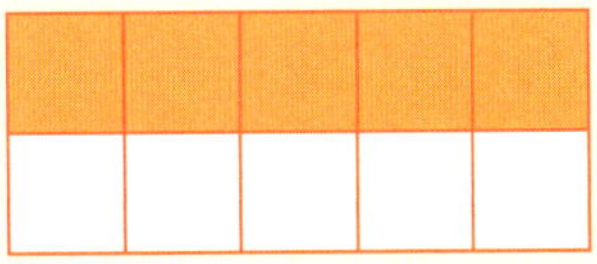

fraction

decimal

9

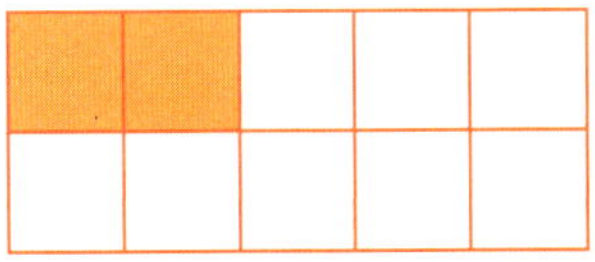

fraction

decimal

Decimal Fractions

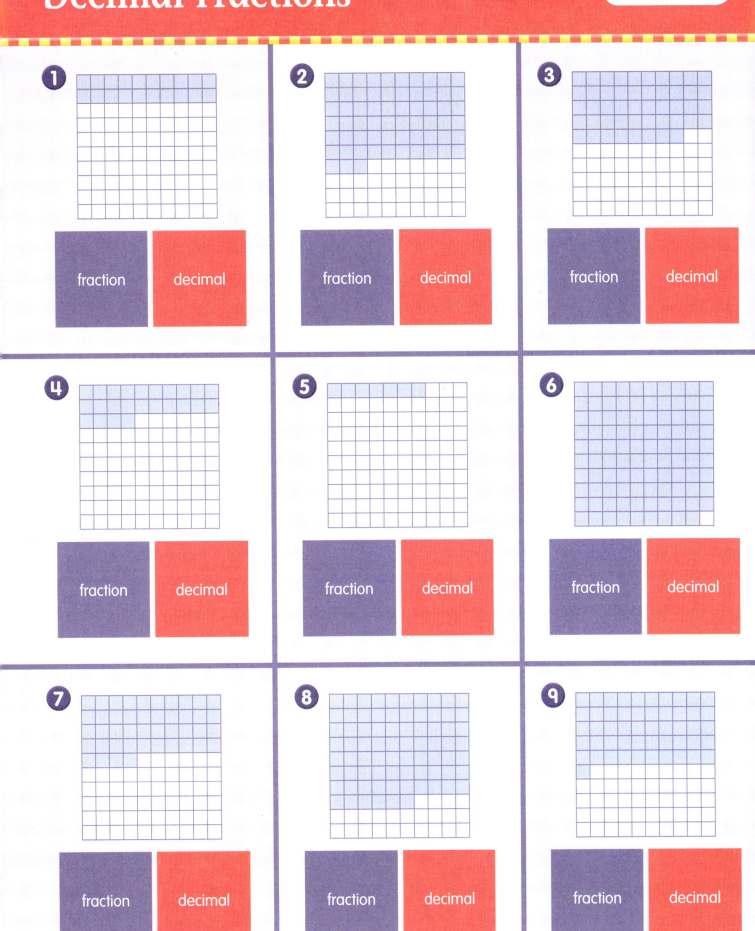

100 frame

1

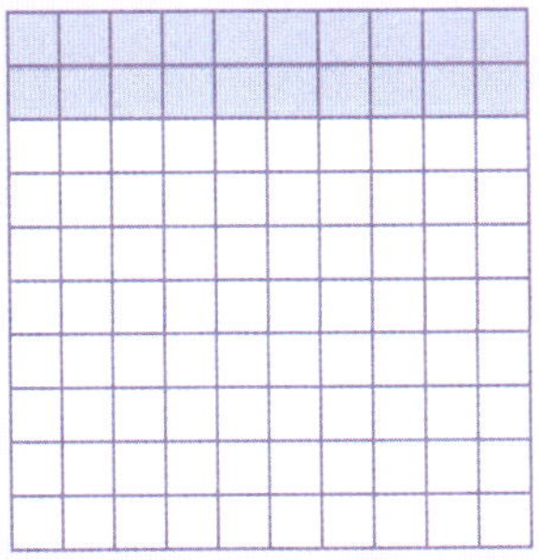

fraction

decimal

2

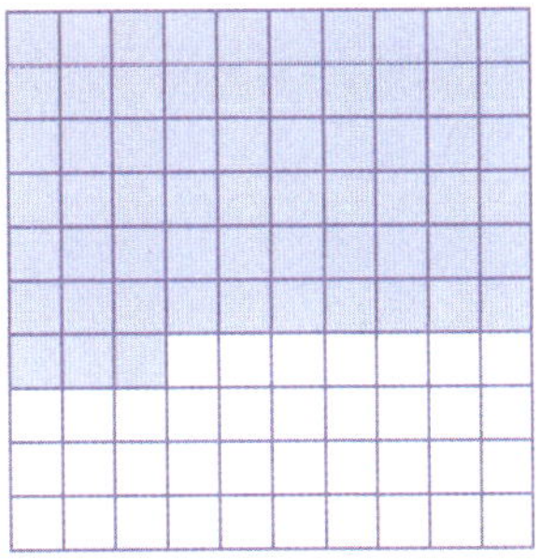

fraction

decimal

3

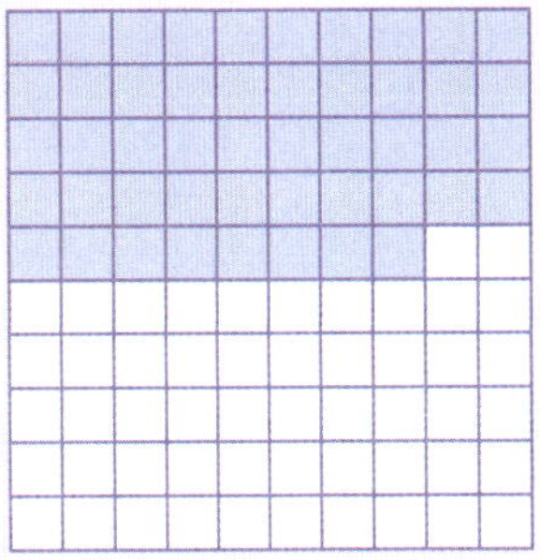

fraction

decimal

4

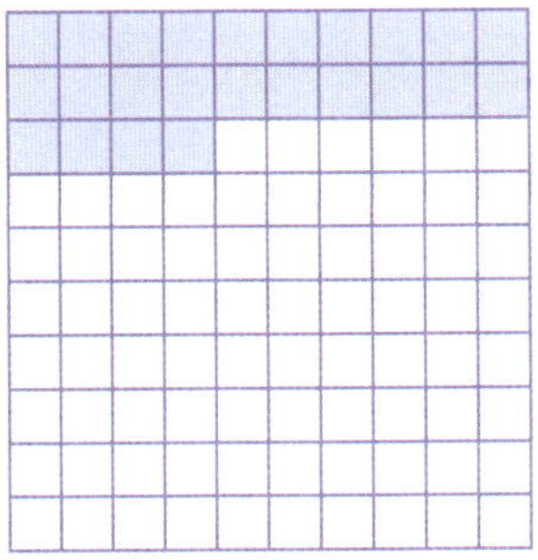

fraction

decimal

5

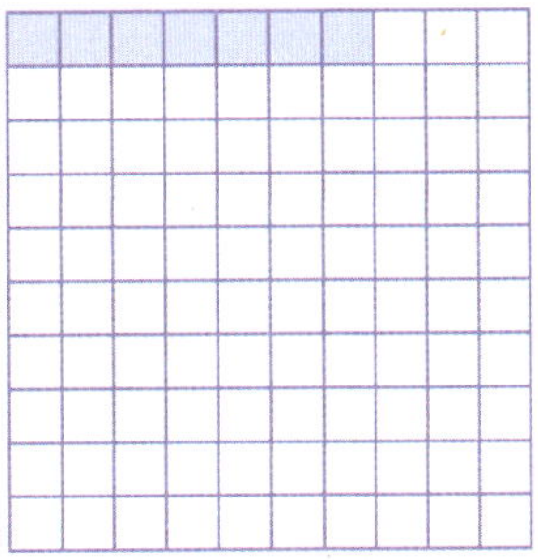

fraction

decimal

6

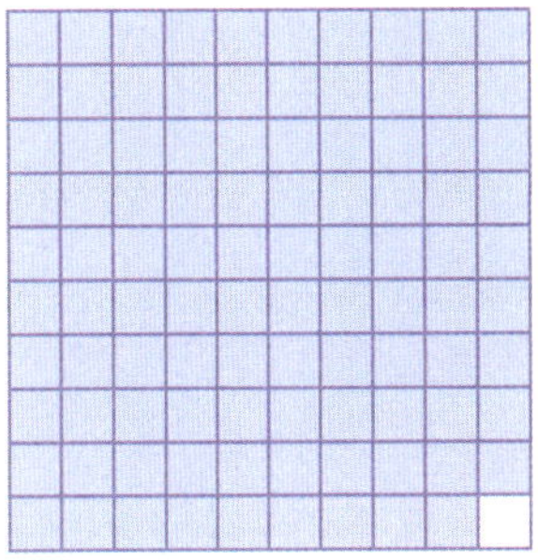

fraction

decimal

7

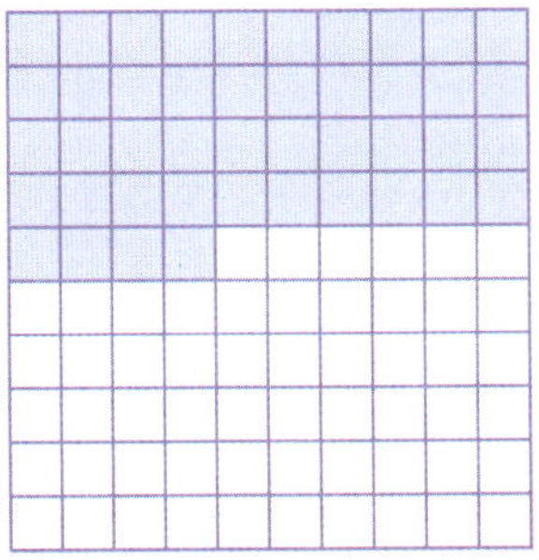

fraction

decimal

8

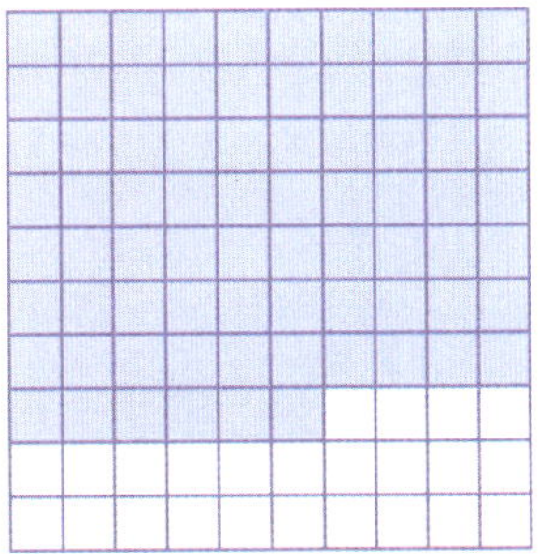

fraction

decimal

9

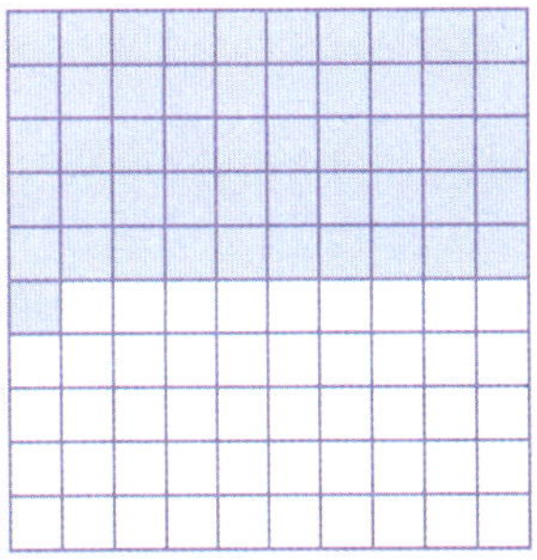

fraction

decimal

$\frac{1}{10}$	$\frac{2}{10}$	$\frac{3}{10}$	$\frac{4}{10}$	$\frac{5}{10}$	$\frac{6}{10}$
$\frac{7}{10}$	$\frac{8}{10}$	$\frac{9}{10}$	$\frac{20}{100}$	$\frac{63}{100}$	$\frac{48}{100}$
$\frac{24}{100}$	$\frac{7}{100}$	$\frac{99}{100}$	$\frac{44}{100}$	$\frac{76}{100}$	$\frac{51}{100}$
0.1	0.2	0.3	0.4	0.5	0.6
0.7	0.8	0.9	0.2	0.63	0.48
0.24	0.07	0.99	0.44	0.76	0.51

Decimal Fractions EMC 3074 © Evan-Moor Corp.	Decimal Fractions EMC 3074 © Evan-Moor Corp.	Decimal Fractions EMC 3074 © Evan-Moor Corp.	Decimal Fractions EMC 3074 © Evan-Moor Corp.	Decimal Fractions EMC 3074 © Evan-Moor Corp.	Decimal Fractions EMC 3074 © Evan-Moor Corp.
Decimal Fractions EMC 3074 © Evan-Moor Corp.	Decimal Fractions EMC 3074 © Evan-Moor Corp.	Decimal Fractions EMC 3074 © Evan-Moor Corp.	Decimal Fractions EMC 3074 © Evan-Moor Corp.	Decimal Fractions EMC 3074 © Evan-Moor Corp.	Decimal Fractions EMC 3074 © Evan-Moor Corp.
Decimal Fractions EMC 3074 © Evan-Moor Corp.	Decimal Fractions EMC 3074 © Evan-Moor Corp.	Decimal Fractions EMC 3074 © Evan-Moor Corp.	Decimal Fractions EMC 3074 © Evan-Moor Corp.	Decimal Fractions EMC 3074 © Evan-Moor Corp.	Decimal Fractions EMC 3074 © Evan-Moor Corp.
Decimal Fractions EMC 3074 © Evan-Moor Corp.	Decimal Fractions EMC 3074 © Evan-Moor Corp.	Decimal Fractions EMC 3074 © Evan-Moor Corp.	Decimal Fractions EMC 3074 © Evan-Moor Corp.	Decimal Fractions EMC 3074 © Evan-Moor Corp.	Decimal Fractions EMC 3074 © Evan-Moor Corp.
Decimal Fractions EMC 3074 © Evan-Moor Corp.	Decimal Fractions EMC 3074 © Evan-Moor Corp.	Decimal Fractions EMC 3074 © Evan-Moor Corp.	Decimal Fractions EMC 3074 © Evan-Moor Corp.	Decimal Fractions EMC 3074 © Evan-Moor Corp.	Decimal Fractions EMC 3074 © Evan-Moor Corp.
Decimal Fractions EMC 3074 © Evan-Moor Corp.	Decimal Fractions EMC 3074 © Evan-Moor Corp.	Decimal Fractions EMC 3074 © Evan-Moor Corp.	Decimal Fractions EMC 3074 © Evan-Moor Corp.	Decimal Fractions EMC 3074 © Evan-Moor Corp.	Decimal Fractions EMC 3074 © Evan-Moor Corp.

Take It to Your Seat Centers

Multiplication Speed Drill

* This center also requires a timer.

Skill: Build fluency with multiplication facts to 12

Steps to Follow

1. **Prepare the center.** (See page 3.) Make sure that students have access to a timer.
2. **Introduce the center.** State the goal. Say: *You will work as quickly as you can to find the products on the mats for the multiplication facts on the cards. Use the Multiplication Table provided if you need help.*
3. **Teach the skill.** Demonstrate how to use the center with individual students or small groups.
4. **Practice the skill.** Have students use the center independently or with a partner.

Contents

Name ____________________ Skill: Build fluency with multiplication facts to 12

Multiplication Speed Drill

I did the activity _____ times.

I used the multiplication table. ☐ **yes** ☐ **no**

I beat the timer. ☐ **yes** ☐ **no**

★ I need to practice these facts.

★ ★ I need to practice these facts.

Multiplication Speed Drill

Skill: Build fluency with multiplication facts to 12

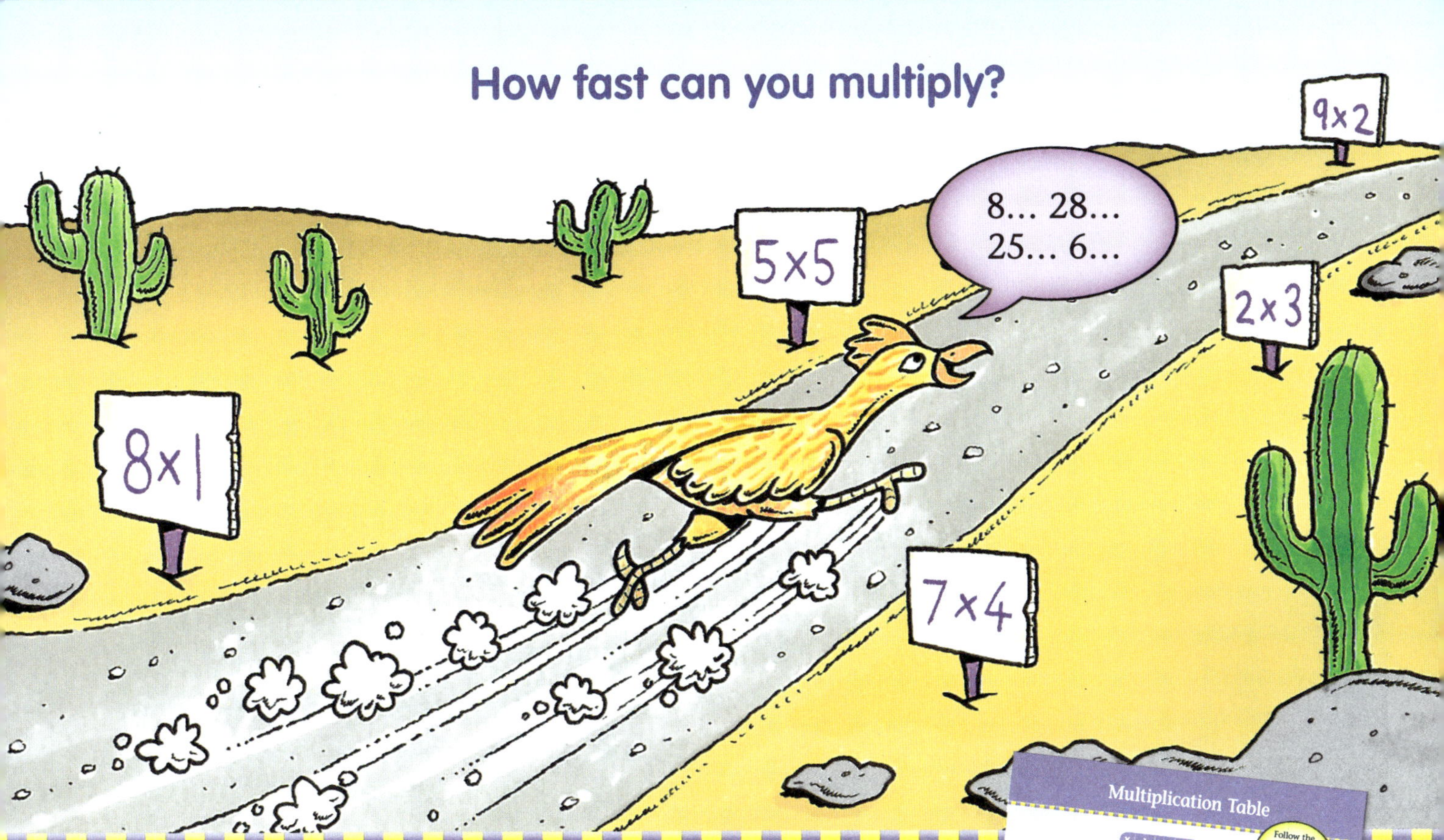

1. Lay out the mat and the Multiplication Table.
2. Start the timer.
3. Read the multiplication fact on each card and find the product on the mat as fast as you can.
4. Place the card over the product. When all the products are covered, look at the number on the back of each card to check your answers.
5. Complete the response form.

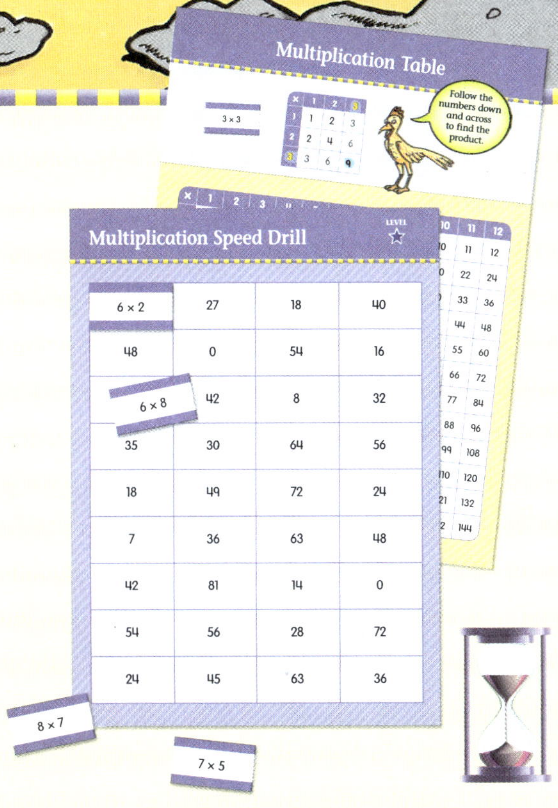

* This center also requires a timer.

Answer Key

Multiplication Speed Drill

(fold)

Response Form

Multiplication Speed Drill

I did the activity ____ times.

I used the multiplication table. ☐ yes ☐ no

I beat the timer. ☐ yes ☐ no

Answers will vary.

★ I need to practice these facts.

★★ I need to practice these facts.

Answer Key

Multiplication Speed Drill

Placement of cards with the same products (9 × 2, 6 × 3, etc.) and cards with inverse equations (6 × 8, 8 × 6; 7 × 9, 9 × 7, etc.) will vary.

Multiplication Speed Drill

LEVEL ☆

6 × 2	9 × 3	9 × 2	8 × 5
8 × 6	6 × 0	9 × 6	8 × 2
7 × 3	7 × 6	8 × 1	8 × 4
7 × 5	6 × 5	8 × 8	8 × 7
6 × 3	7 × 7	9 × 8	8 × 3
7 × 1	9 × 4	9 × 7	6 × 8
6 × 7	9 × 9	7 × 2	9 × 0
6 × 9	7 × 8	7 × 4	8 × 9
6 × 4	9 × 5	7 × 9	6 × 6

Multiplication Speed Drill

LEVEL ☆☆

10 × 2	11 × 7	12 × 3	12 × 9
11 × 3	10 × 4	12 × 1	12 × 5
10 × 11	11 × 5	10 × 9	11 × 1
12 × 7	10 × 3	11 × 12	12 × 2
10 × 5	10 × 1	10 × 0	12 × 4
10 × 13	11 × 4	10 × 12	10 × 8
11 × 2	12 × 8	10 × 7	11 × 11
10 × 10	11 × 0	11 × 6	11 × 9
12 × 6	11 × 8	12 × 0	12 × 12

Multiplication Table

3 × 3

×	1	2	3
1	1	2	3
2	2	4	6
3	3	6	9

Follow the numbers down and across to find the product.

×	1	2	3	4	5	6	7	8	9	10	11	12
1	1	2	3	4	5	6	7	8	9	10	11	12
2	2	4	6	8	10	12	14	16	18	20	22	24
3	3	6	9	12	15	18	21	24	27	30	33	36
4	4	8	12	16	20	24	28	32	36	40	44	48
5	5	10	15	20	25	30	35	40	45	50	55	60
6	6	12	18	24	30	36	42	48	54	60	66	72
7	7	14	21	28	35	42	49	56	63	70	77	84
8	8	16	24	32	40	48	56	64	72	80	88	96
9	9	18	27	36	45	54	63	72	81	90	99	108
10	10	20	30	40	50	60	70	80	90	100	110	120
11	11	22	33	44	55	66	77	88	99	110	121	132
12	12	24	36	48	60	72	84	96	108	120	132	144

Multiplication Speed Drill

LEVEL ★

12	27	18	40
48	0	54	16
21	42	8	32
35	30	64	56
18	49	72	24
7	36	63	48
42	81	14	0
54	56	28	72
24	45	63	36

Multiplication Speed Drill

LEVEL ★★

20	77	36	108
33	40	12	60
110	55	90	11
84	30	132	24
50	10	0	48
130	44	120	80
22	96	70	121
100	0	66	99
72	88	0	144

6 × 2	7 × 4	8 × 5	9 × 6
6 × 3	7 × 5	8 × 6	9 × 7
6 × 4	7 × 6	8 × 7	9 × 8
6 × 5	7 × 7	8 × 8	9 × 9
6 × 6	7 × 8	8 × 9	9 × 2
6 × 7	7 × 9	9 × 0	8 × 2
6 × 8	8 × 1	9 × 3	7 × 3
6 × 9	8 × 3	9 × 4	6 × 0
7 × 2	8 × 4	9 × 5	7 × 1

54 Multiplication Speed Drill EMC 3074 • © Evan-Moor Corp.	40 Multiplication Speed Drill EMC 3074 • © Evan-Moor Corp.	28 Multiplication Speed Drill EMC 3074 • © Evan-Moor Corp.	12 Multiplication Speed Drill EMC 3074 • © Evan-Moor Corp.
63 Multiplication Speed Drill EMC 3074 • © Evan-Moor Corp.	48 Multiplication Speed Drill EMC 3074 • © Evan-Moor Corp.	35 Multiplication Speed Drill EMC 3074 • © Evan-Moor Corp.	18 Multiplication Speed Drill EMC 3074 • © Evan-Moor Corp.
72 Multiplication Speed Drill EMC 3074 • © Evan-Moor Corp.	56 Multiplication Speed Drill EMC 3074 • © Evan-Moor Corp.	42 Multiplication Speed Drill EMC 3074 • © Evan-Moor Corp.	24 Multiplication Speed Drill EMC 3074 • © Evan-Moor Corp.
81 Multiplication Speed Drill EMC 3074 • © Evan-Moor Corp.	64 Multiplication Speed Drill EMC 3074 • © Evan-Moor Corp.	49 Multiplication Speed Drill EMC 3074 • © Evan-Moor Corp.	30 Multiplication Speed Drill EMC 3074 • © Evan-Moor Corp.
18 Multiplication Speed Drill EMC 3074 • © Evan-Moor Corp.	72 Multiplication Speed Drill EMC 3074 • © Evan-Moor Corp.	56 Multiplication Speed Drill EMC 3074 • © Evan-Moor Corp.	36 Multiplication Speed Drill EMC 3074 • © Evan-Moor Corp.
16 Multiplication Speed Drill EMC 3074 • © Evan-Moor Corp.	0 Multiplication Speed Drill EMC 3074 • © Evan-Moor Corp.	63 Multiplication Speed Drill EMC 3074 • © Evan-Moor Corp.	42 Multiplication Speed Drill EMC 3074 • © Evan-Moor Corp.
21 Multiplication Speed Drill EMC 3074 • © Evan-Moor Corp.	27 Multiplication Speed Drill EMC 3074 • © Evan-Moor Corp.	8 Multiplication Speed Drill EMC 3074 • © Evan-Moor Corp.	48 Multiplication Speed Drill EMC 3074 • © Evan-Moor Corp.
0 Multiplication Speed Drill EMC 3074 • © Evan-Moor Corp.	36 Multiplication Speed Drill EMC 3074 • © Evan-Moor Corp.	24 Multiplication Speed Drill EMC 3074 • © Evan-Moor Corp.	54 Multiplication Speed Drill EMC 3074 • © Evan-Moor Corp.
7 Multiplication Speed Drill EMC 3074 • © Evan-Moor Corp.	45 Multiplication Speed Drill EMC 3074 • © Evan-Moor Corp.	32 Multiplication Speed Drill EMC 3074 • © Evan-Moor Corp.	14 Multiplication Speed Drill EMC 3074 • © Evan-Moor Corp.

10 × 0	10 × 10	11 × 6	12 × 3
10 × 1	10 × 11	11 × 7	12 × 4
10 × 2	10 × 12	11 × 8	12 × 5
10 × 3	11 × 0	11 × 9	12 × 6
10 × 4	11 × 1	11 × 11	12 × 7
10 × 5	11 × 2	11 × 12	12 × 8
10 × 7	11 × 3	12 × 0	12 × 9
10 × 8	11 × 4	12 × 1	10 × 13
10 × 9	11 × 5	12 × 2	12 × 12

36 Multiplication Speed Drill EMC 3074 • © Evan-Moor Corp.	66 Multiplication Speed Drill EMC 3074 • © Evan-Moor Corp.	100 Multiplication Speed Drill EMC 3074 • © Evan-Moor Corp.	0 Multiplication Speed Drill EMC 3074 • © Evan-Moor Corp.
48 Multiplication Speed Drill EMC 3074 • © Evan-Moor Corp.	77 Multiplication Speed Drill EMC 3074 • © Evan-Moor Corp.	110 Multiplication Speed Drill EMC 3074 • © Evan-Moor Corp.	10 Multiplication Speed Drill EMC 3074 • © Evan-Moor Corp.
60 Multiplication Speed Drill EMC 3074 • © Evan-Moor Corp.	88 Multiplication Speed Drill EMC 3074 • © Evan-Moor Corp.	120 Multiplication Speed Drill EMC 3074 • © Evan-Moor Corp.	20 Multiplication Speed Drill EMC 3074 • © Evan-Moor Corp.
72 Multiplication Speed Drill EMC 3074 • © Evan-Moor Corp.	99 Multiplication Speed Drill EMC 3074 • © Evan-Moor Corp.	0 Multiplication Speed Drill EMC 3074 • © Evan-Moor Corp.	30 Multiplication Speed Drill EMC 3074 • © Evan-Moor Corp.
84 Multiplication Speed Drill EMC 3074 • © Evan-Moor Corp.	121 Multiplication Speed Drill EMC 3074 • © Evan-Moor Corp.	11 Multiplication Speed Drill EMC 3074 • © Evan-Moor Corp.	40 Multiplication Speed Drill EMC 3074 • © Evan-Moor Corp.
96 Multiplication Speed Drill EMC 3074 • © Evan-Moor Corp.	132 Multiplication Speed Drill EMC 3074 • © Evan-Moor Corp.	22 Multiplication Speed Drill EMC 3074 • © Evan-Moor Corp.	50 Multiplication Speed Drill EMC 3074 • © Evan-Moor Corp.
108 Multiplication Speed Drill EMC 3074 • © Evan-Moor Corp.	0 Multiplication Speed Drill EMC 3074 • © Evan-Moor Corp.	33 Multiplication Speed Drill EMC 3074 • © Evan-Moor Corp.	70 Multiplication Speed Drill EMC 3074 • © Evan-Moor Corp.
130 Multiplication Speed Drill EMC 3074 • © Evan-Moor Corp.	12 Multiplication Speed Drill EMC 3074 • © Evan-Moor Corp.	44 Multiplication Speed Drill EMC 3074 • © Evan-Moor Corp.	80 Multiplication Speed Drill EMC 3074 • © Evan-Moor Corp.
144 Multiplication Speed Drill EMC 3074 • © Evan-Moor Corp.	24 Multiplication Speed Drill EMC 3074 • © Evan-Moor Corp.	55 Multiplication Speed Drill EMC 3074 • © Evan-Moor Corp.	90 Multiplication Speed Drill EMC 3074 • © Evan-Moor Corp.

Take It to Your Seat Centers

Multistep Word Problems

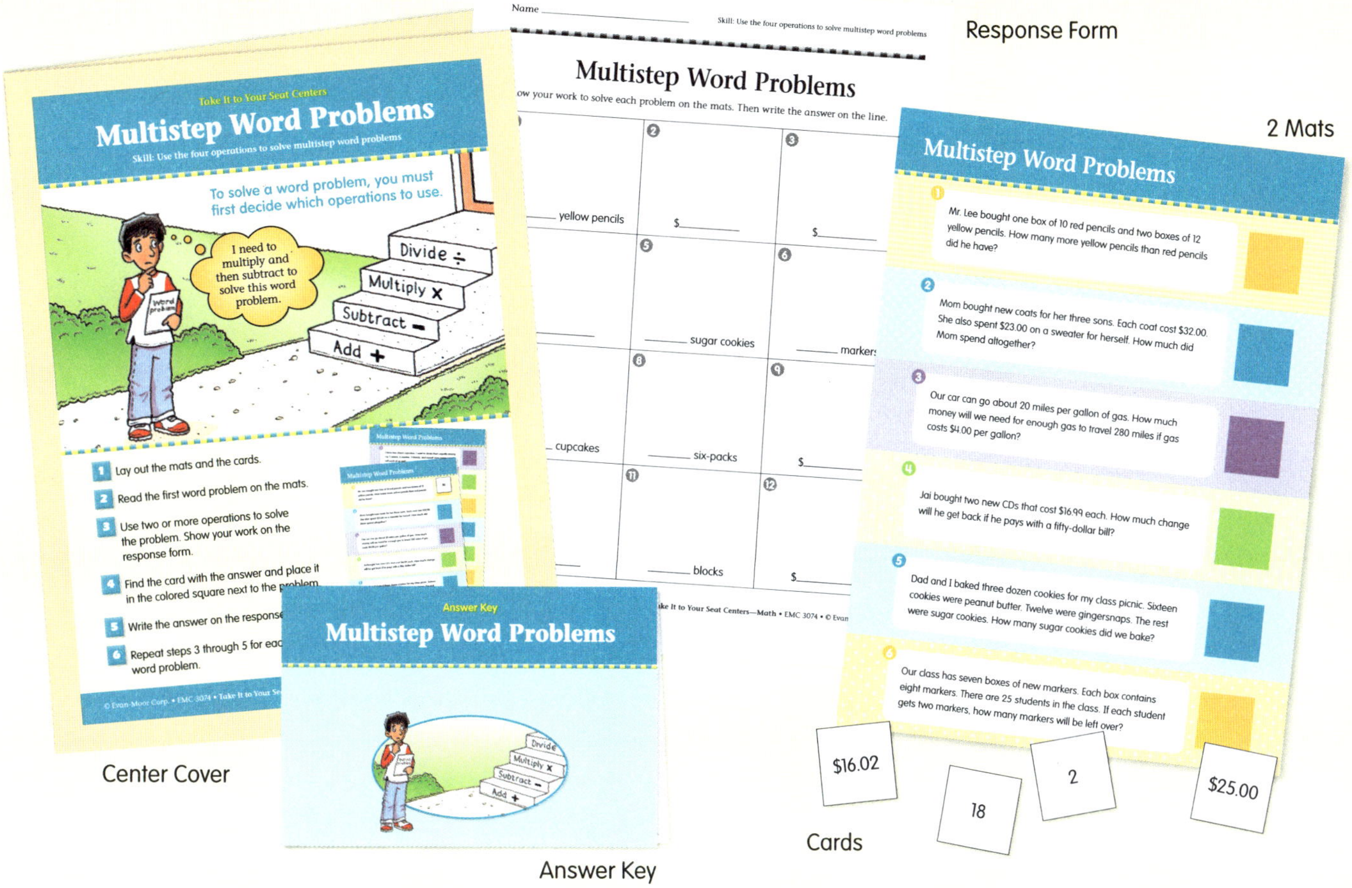

Skill: Use the four operations to solve multistep word problems

Steps to Follow

1. **Prepare the center.** (See page 3.)
2. **Introduce the center.** State the goal. Say: *You will read and solve word problems that require more than one operation.*
3. **Teach the skill.** Demonstrate how to use the center with individual students or small groups.
4. **Practice the skill.** Have students use the center independently or with a partner.

Contents

Name ______________________ Skill: Use the four operations to solve multistep word problems

Multistep Word Problems

Show your work to solve each problem on the mats. Then write the answer on the line.

1 ______ yellow pencils	2 $______	3 $______
4 $______	5 ______ sugar cookies	6 ______ markers
7 ______ cupcakes	8 ______ six-packs	9 $______
10 $______	11 ______ blocks	12 $______

Multistep Word Problems

Skill: Use the four operations to solve multistep word problems

To solve a word problem, you must first decide which operations to use.

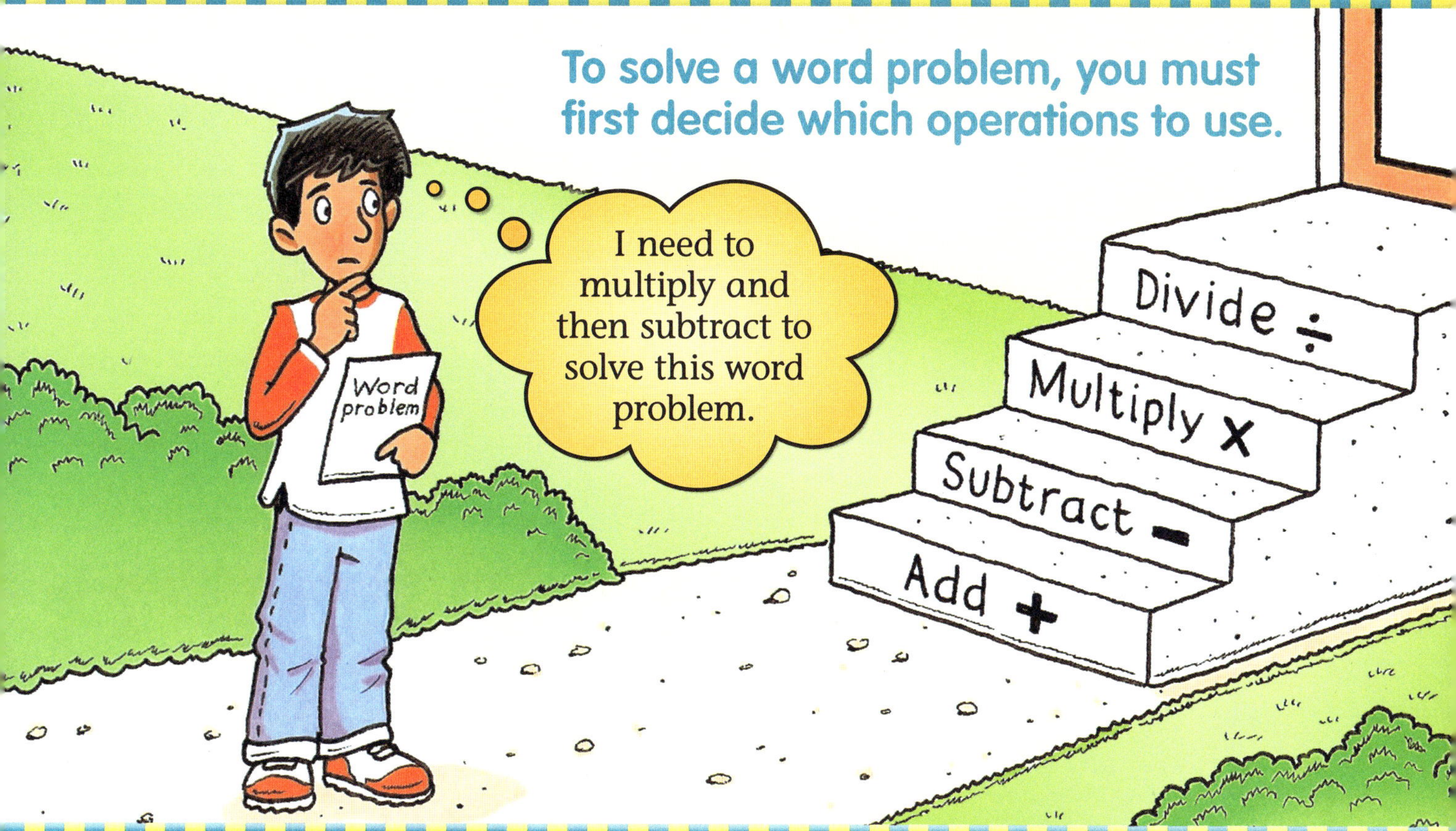

1. Lay out the mats and the cards.
2. Read the first word problem on the mats.
3. Use two or more operations to solve the problem. Show your work on the response form.
4. Find the card with the answer and place it in the colored square next to the problem.
5. Write the answer on the response form.
6. Repeat steps 3 through 5 for each word problem.

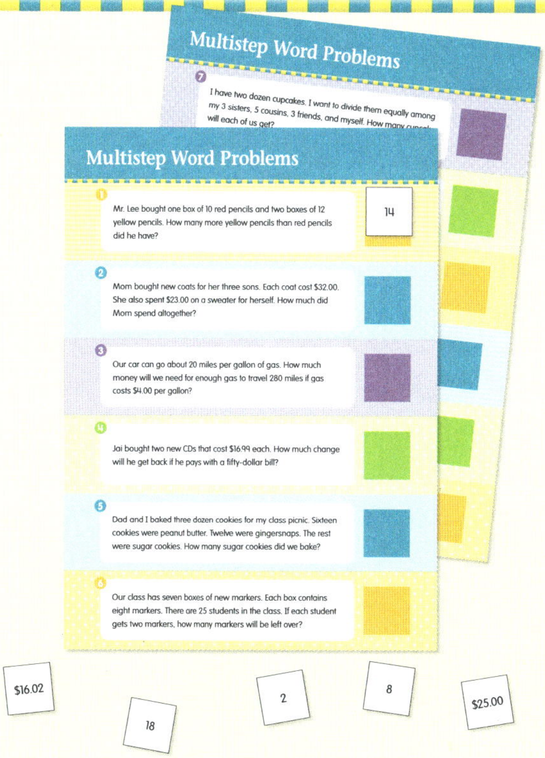

(fold)

Answer Key

Multistep Word Problems

Response Form

Multistep Word Problems

Show your work to solve each problem on the mats. Then write the answer on the line.

1 14 yellow pencils	2 $ 119.00	3 $ 56.00
4 $ 16.02	5 8 sugar cookies	6 6 markers
7 2 cupcakes	8 3 six-packs	9 $ 8.40
10 $ 56.10	11 20 blocks	12 $ 25.00

Answer Key

Multistep Word Problems

Multistep Word Problems

1. Mr. Lee bought one box of 10 red pencils and two boxes of 12 yellow pencils. How many more yellow pencils than red pencils did he have? **14**

2. Mom bought new coats for her three sons. Each coat cost $32.00. She also spent $23.00 on a sweater for herself. How much did Mom spend altogether? **$119.00**

3. Our car can go about 20 miles per gallon of gas. How much money will we need for enough gas to travel 280 miles if gas costs $4.00 per gallon? **$56.00**

4. Jai bought two new CDs that cost $16.99 each. How much change will he get back if he pays with a fifty-dollar bill? **$16.02**

5. Dad and I baked three dozen cookies for my class picnic. Sixteen cookies were peanut butter. Twelve were gingersnaps. The rest were sugar cookies. How many sugar cookies did we bake? **8**

6. Our class has seven boxes of new markers. Each box contains eight markers. There are 25 students in the class. If each student gets two markers, how many markers will be left over? **6**

Multistep Word Problems

7. I have two dozen cupcakes. I want to divide them equally among my 3 sisters, 5 cousins, 3 friends, and myself. How many cupcakes will each of us get? **2**

8. Amy wants nine rows of flowers in her garden with eight plants in each row. She bought 9 six-packs of flower plants. How many more six-packs of plants does she need? **3**

9. Naomi and her four sisters earned $18.00 for baby-sitting on Friday and $24.00 on Saturday. How much will each girl receive if they divide their earnings equally? **$8.40**

10. Jose's mom bought two cases of ice-cream bars for his birthday party. Each case cost $24.30. She also bought six liters of cola. Each liter cost $1.25. How much did Jose's mom spend altogether? **$56.10**

11. Sally walks 9 blocks to school and 9 blocks back home five days a week. Ahmed walks 7 blocks to school and 7 blocks back home five days a week. How many more blocks does Sally walk each week than Ahmed? **20**

12. The 205 students at Lincoln Elementary School are raising money for new playground equipment. Their goal is $5,625.00. If 100 students each raise $30.00, how much will each of the other students need to raise to meet the goal? **$25.00**

Multistep Word Problems

1. Mr. Lee bought one box of 10 red pencils and two boxes of 12 yellow pencils. How many more yellow pencils than red pencils did he have?

2. Mom bought new coats for her three sons. Each coat cost $32.00. She also spent $23.00 on a sweater for herself. How much did Mom spend altogether?

3. Our car can go about 20 miles per gallon of gas. How much money will we need for enough gas to travel 280 miles if gas costs $4.00 per gallon?

4. Jai bought two new CDs that cost $16.99 each. How much change will he get back if he pays with a fifty-dollar bill?

5. Dad and I baked three dozen cookies for my class picnic. Sixteen cookies were peanut butter. Twelve were gingersnaps. The rest were sugar cookies. How many sugar cookies did we bake?

6. Our class has seven boxes of new markers. Each box contains eight markers. There are 25 students in the class. If each student gets two markers, how many markers will be left over?

Multistep Word Problems

7. I have two dozen cupcakes. I want to divide them equally among my 3 sisters, 5 cousins, 3 friends, and myself. How many cupcakes will each of us get?

8. Amy wants nine rows of flowers in her garden with eight plants in each row. She bought 9 six-packs of flower plants. How many more six-packs of plants does she need?

9. Naomi and her four sisters earned $18.00 for baby-sitting on Friday and $24.00 on Saturday. How much will each girl receive if they divide their earnings equally?

10. Jose's mom bought two cases of ice-cream bars for his birthday party. Each case cost $24.30. She also bought six liters of cola. Each liter cost $1.25. How much did Jose's mom spend altogether?

11. Sally walks 9 blocks to school and 9 blocks back home five days a week. Ahmed walks 7 blocks to school and 7 blocks back home five days a week. How many more blocks does Sally walk each week than Ahmed?

12. The 205 students at Lincoln Elementary School are raising money for new playground equipment. Their goal is $5,625.00. If 100 students each raise $30.00, how much will each of the other students need to raise to meet the goal?

1	2	3	4	5
6	7	8	9	10
11	12	13	14	15
16	17	18	19	20
21	22	23	24	25
$8.40	$25.00	$16.02	$56.00	$56.10
$7.50	$20.00	$34.99	$53.00	$55.50
$9.20	$35.00	$43.01	$46.00	$51.60
$119.00	$116.00	$113.00		

Multistep Word Problems EMC 3074 © Evan-Moor Corp.	Multistep Word Problems EMC 3074 © Evan-Moor Corp.	Multistep Word Problems EMC 3074 © Evan-Moor Corp.	Multistep Word Problems EMC 3074 © Evan-Moor Corp.	Multistep Word Problems EMC 3074 © Evan-Moor Corp.
Multistep Word Problems EMC 3074 © Evan-Moor Corp.	Multistep Word Problems EMC 3074 © Evan-Moor Corp.	Multistep Word Problems EMC 3074 © Evan-Moor Corp.	Multistep Word Problems EMC 3074 © Evan-Moor Corp.	Multistep Word Problems EMC 3074 © Evan-Moor Corp.
Multistep Word Problems EMC 3074 © Evan-Moor Corp.	Multistep Word Problems EMC 3074 © Evan-Moor Corp.	Multistep Word Problems EMC 3074 © Evan-Moor Corp.	Multistep Word Problems EMC 3074 © Evan-Moor Corp.	Multistep Word Problems EMC 3074 © Evan-Moor Corp.
Multistep Word Problems EMC 3074 © Evan-Moor Corp.	Multistep Word Problems EMC 3074 © Evan-Moor Corp.	Multistep Word Problems EMC 3074 © Evan-Moor Corp.	Multistep Word Problems EMC 3074 © Evan-Moor Corp.	Multistep Word Problems EMC 3074 © Evan-Moor Corp.
Multistep Word Problems EMC 3074 © Evan-Moor Corp.	Multistep Word Problems EMC 3074 © Evan-Moor Corp.	Multistep Word Problems EMC 3074 © Evan-Moor Corp.	Multistep Word Problems EMC 3074 © Evan-Moor Corp.	Multistep Word Problems EMC 3074 © Evan-Moor Corp.
Multistep Word Problems EMC 3074 © Evan-Moor Corp.	Multistep Word Problems EMC 3074 © Evan-Moor Corp.	Multistep Word Problems EMC 3074 © Evan-Moor Corp.	Multistep Word Problems EMC 3074 © Evan-Moor Corp.	Multistep Word Problems EMC 3074 © Evan-Moor Corp.
Multistep Word Problems EMC 3074 © Evan-Moor Corp.	Multistep Word Problems EMC 3074 © Evan-Moor Corp.	Multistep Word Problems EMC 3074 © Evan-Moor Corp.	Multistep Word Problems EMC 3074 © Evan-Moor Corp.	Multistep Word Problems EMC 3074 © Evan-Moor Corp.
Multistep Word Problems EMC 3074 © Evan-Moor Corp.	Multistep Word Problems EMC 3074 © Evan-Moor Corp.	Multistep Word Problems EMC 3074 © Evan-Moor Corp.	Multistep Word Problems EMC 3074 © Evan-Moor Corp.	Multistep Word Problems EMC 3074 © Evan-Moor Corp.
		Multistep Word Problems EMC 3074 © Evan-Moor Corp.	Multistep Word Problems EMC 3074 © Evan-Moor Corp.	Multistep Word Problems EMC 3074 © Evan-Moor Corp.

Units of Length

Written Practice

Length Measurements

2 Mats

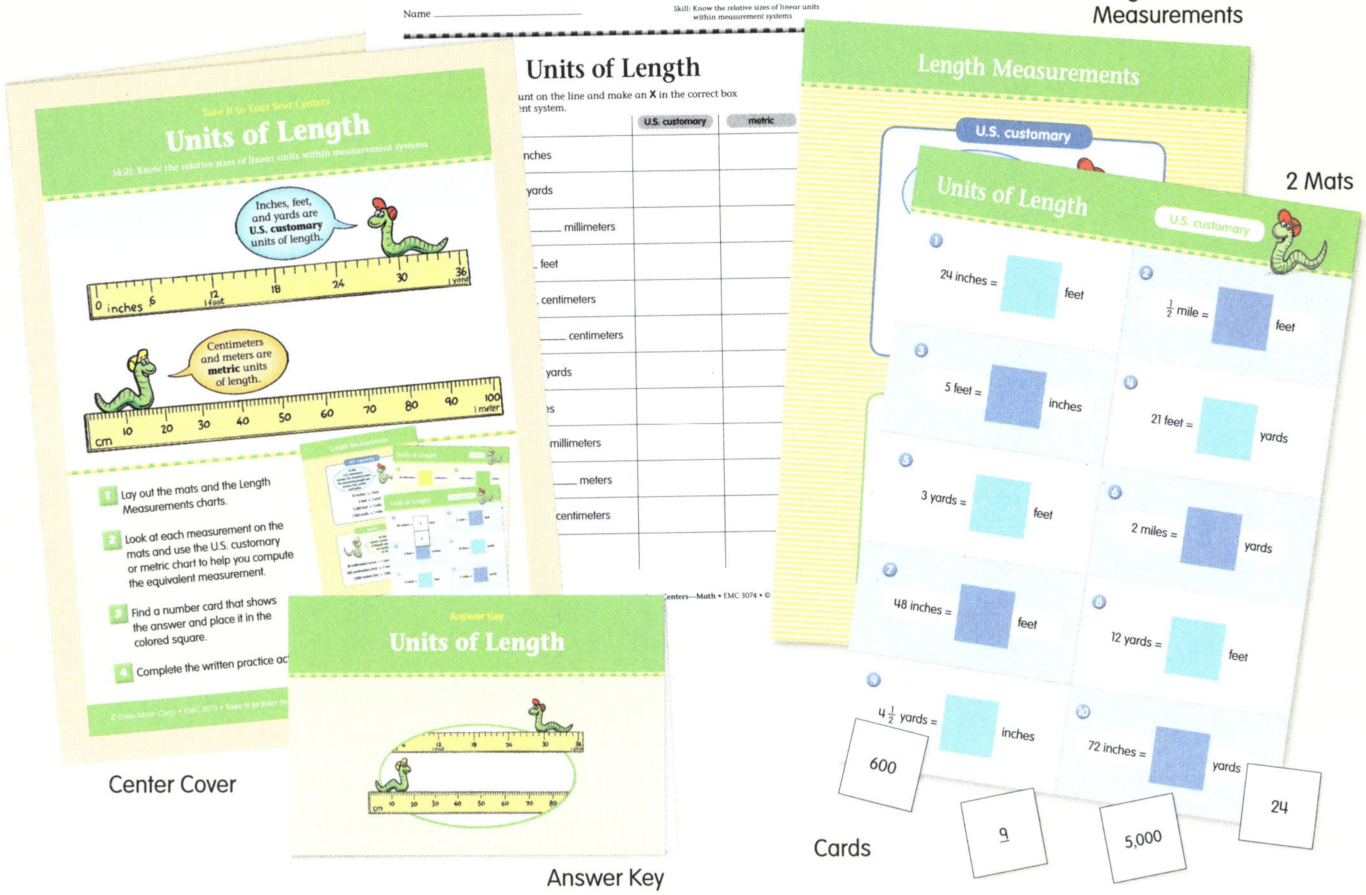

Center Cover

Answer Key

Cards

Skill: Know the relative sizes of linear units within measurement systems (U.S. customary and metric)

Steps to Follow

1. **Prepare the center.** (See page 3.)
2. **Introduce the center.** State the goal. Say: *You will compute equivalent measurements of length in the U.S. customary and metric systems.*
3. **Teach the skill.** Demonstrate how to use the center with individual students or small groups.
4. **Practice the skill.** Have students use the center independently or with a partner.

Contents

Name ______________________

Skill: Know the relative sizes of linear units within measurement systems

Units of Length

Write the equivalent amount on the line and make an **X** in the correct box to identify the measurement system.

	U.S. customary	metric
1 yard = __________ inches		
$\frac{1}{2}$ mile = __________ yards		
80 centimeters = __________ millimeters		
36 inches = __________ feet		
10 meters = __________ centimeters		
600 millimeters = __________ centimeters		
180 inches = __________ yards		
6 feet = __________ inches		
$2\frac{1}{2}$ meters = __________ millimeters		
2,000 millimeters = __________ meters		
$\frac{1}{10}$ kilometer = __________ centimeters		
12 feet = __________ yards		

Units of Length

Skill: Know the relative sizes of linear units within measurement systems

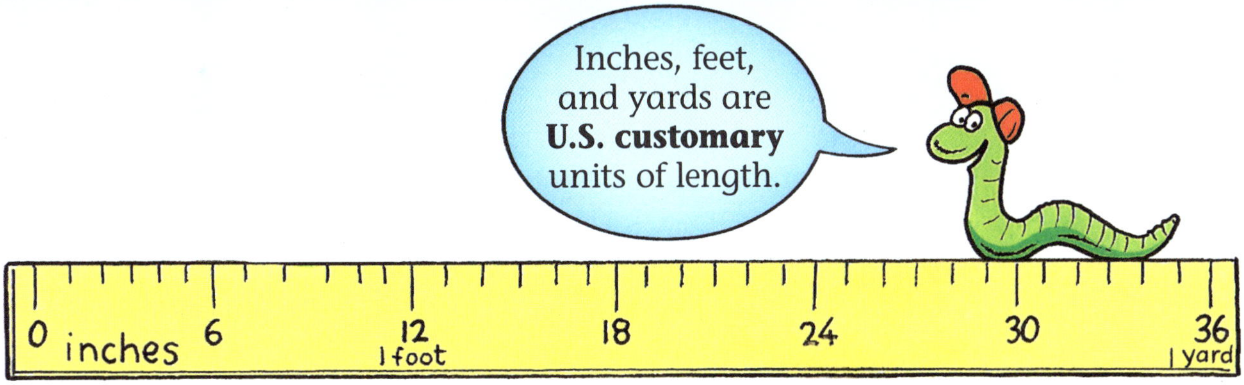

1. Lay out the mats and the Length Measurements charts.
2. Look at each measurement on the mats and use the U.S. customary or metric chart to help you compute the equivalent measurement.
3. Find a number card that shows the answer and place it in the colored square.
4. Complete the written practice activity.

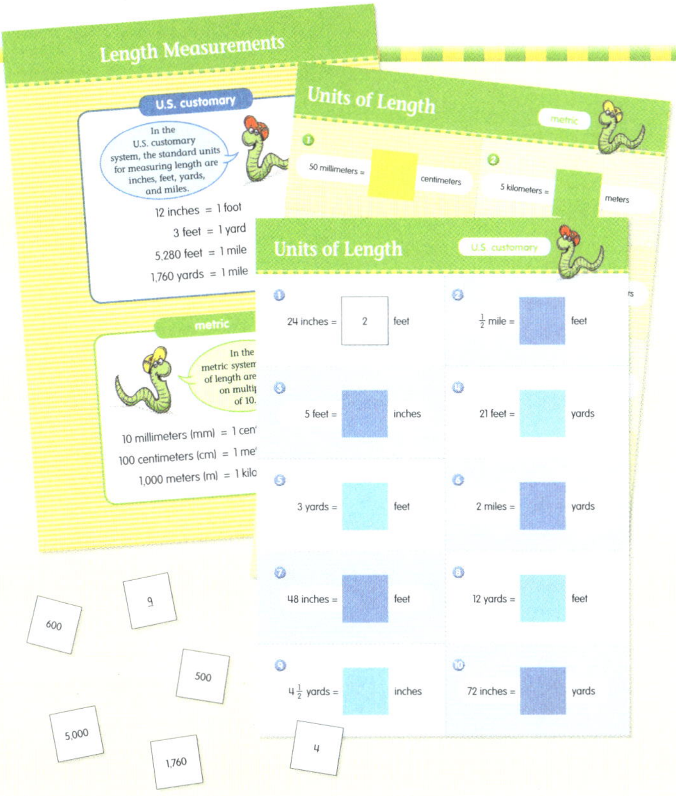

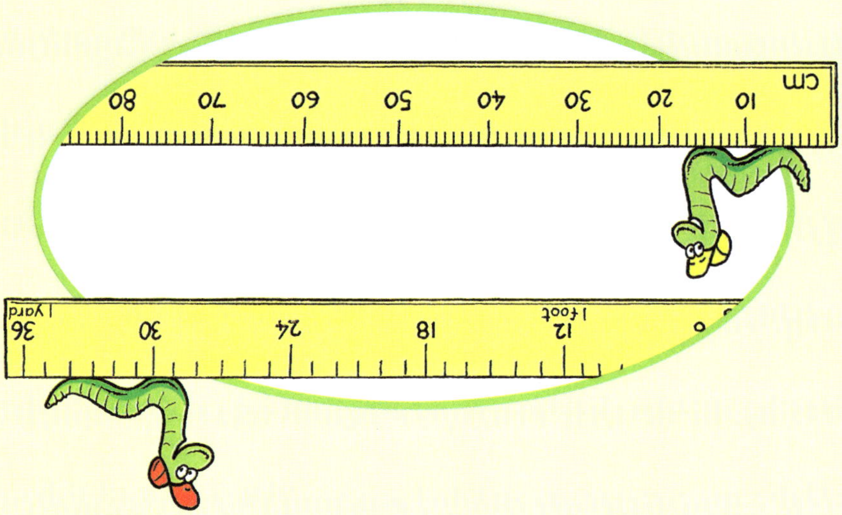

Answer Key

Units of Length

(fold)

Written Practice

Units of Length

Write the equivalent amount on the line and make an **X** in the correct box to identify the measurement system.

	U.S. customary	metric
1 yard = 36 inches	X	
$\frac{1}{2}$ mile = 880 yards	X	
80 centimeters = 800 millimeters		X
36 inches = 3 feet	X	
10 meters = 1,000 centimeters		X
600 millimeters = 60 centimeters		X
180 inches = 5 yards	X	
6 feet = 72 inches	X	
$2\frac{1}{2}$ meters = 2,500 millimeters		X
2,000 millimeters = 2 meters		X
$\frac{1}{10}$ kilometer = 10,000 centimeters		X
12 feet = 4 yards	X	

Answer Key

Units of Length

Units of Length — U.S. customary

1. 24 inches = 2 feet
2. $\frac{1}{2}$ mile = 2,640 feet
3. 5 feet = 60 inches
4. 21 feet = 7 yards
5. 3 yards = 9 feet
6. 2 miles = 3,520 yards
7. 48 inches = 4 feet
8. 12 yards = 36 feet
9. $4\frac{1}{2}$ yards = 162 inches
10. 72 inches = 2 yards

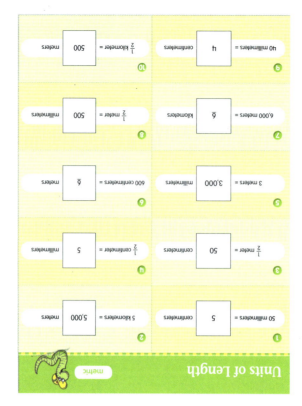

Units of Length — metric

1. 50 millimeters = 5 centimeters
2. 5 kilometers = 5,000 meters
3. $\frac{1}{2}$ meter = 50 centimeters
4. $\frac{1}{2}$ centimeter = 5 millimeters
5. 3 meters = 3,000 millimeters
6. 600 centimeters = 6 meters
7. 6,000 meters = 6 kilometers
8. $\frac{1}{2}$ meter = 500 millimeters
9. 40 millimeters = 4 centimeters
10. $\frac{1}{2}$ kilometer = 500 meters

Length Measurements

U.S. customary

In the U.S. customary system, the standard units for measuring length are inches, feet, yards, and miles.

12 inches = 1 foot

3 feet = 1 yard

5,280 feet = 1 mile

1,760 yards = 1 mile

metric

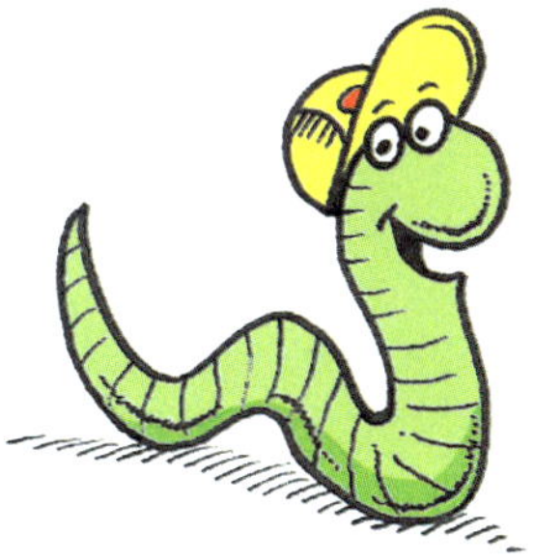

In the metric system, units of length are based on multiples of 10.

10 millimeters (mm) = 1 centimeter (cm)

100 centimeters (cm) = 1 meter (m)

1,000 meters (m) = 1 kilometer (km)

Units of Length

U.S. customary

1. 24 inches = ____ feet

2. $\frac{1}{2}$ mile = ____ feet

3. 5 feet = ____ inches

4. 21 feet = ____ yards

5. 3 yards = ____ feet

6. 2 miles = ____ yards

7. 48 inches = ____ feet

8. 12 yards = ____ feet

9. $4\frac{1}{2}$ yards = ____ inches

10. 72 inches = ____ yards

Units of Length

metric

1. 50 millimeters = ☐ centimeters

2. 5 kilometers = ☐ meters

3. $\frac{1}{2}$ meter = ☐ centimeters

4. $\frac{1}{2}$ centimeter = ☐ millimeters

5. 3 meters = ☐ millimeters

6. 600 centimeters = ☐ meters

7. 6,000 meters = ☐ kilometers

8. $\frac{1}{2}$ meter = ☐ millimeters

9. 40 millimeters = ☐ centimeters

10. $\frac{1}{2}$ kilometer = ☐ meters

2	2	3	3	4	4
5	5	6	6	7	7
8	8	9	9	24	36
50	60	70	80	66	162
186	500	500	600	1,000	1,760
2,000	2,640	3,000	3,520	4,000	5,000

Units of Length EMC 3074 © Evan-Moor Corp.	Units of Length EMC 3074 © Evan-Moor Corp.	Units of Length EMC 3074 © Evan-Moor Corp.	Units of Length EMC 3074 © Evan-Moor Corp.	Units of Length EMC 3074 © Evan-Moor Corp.	Units of Length EMC 3074 © Evan-Moor Corp.
Units of Length EMC 3074 © Evan-Moor Corp.	Units of Length EMC 3074 © Evan-Moor Corp.	Units of Length EMC 3074 © Evan-Moor Corp.	Units of Length EMC 3074 © Evan-Moor Corp.	Units of Length EMC 3074 © Evan-Moor Corp.	Units of Length EMC 3074 © Evan-Moor Corp.
Units of Length EMC 3074 © Evan-Moor Corp.	Units of Length EMC 3074 © Evan-Moor Corp.	Units of Length EMC 3074 © Evan-Moor Corp.	Units of Length EMC 3074 © Evan-Moor Corp.	Units of Length EMC 3074 © Evan-Moor Corp.	Units of Length EMC 3074 © Evan-Moor Corp.
Units of Length EMC 3074 © Evan-Moor Corp.	Units of Length EMC 3074 © Evan-Moor Corp.	Units of Length EMC 3074 © Evan-Moor Corp.	Units of Length EMC 3074 © Evan-Moor Corp.	Units of Length EMC 3074 © Evan-Moor Corp.	Units of Length EMC 3074 © Evan-Moor Corp.
Units of Length EMC 3074 © Evan-Moor Corp.	Units of Length EMC 3074 © Evan-Moor Corp.	Units of Length EMC 3074 © Evan-Moor Corp.	Units of Length EMC 3074 © Evan-Moor Corp.	Units of Length EMC 3074 © Evan-Moor Corp.	Units of Length EMC 3074 © Evan-Moor Corp.
Units of Length EMC 3074 © Evan-Moor Corp.	Units of Length EMC 3074 © Evan-Moor Corp.	Units of Length EMC 3074 © Evan-Moor Corp.	Units of Length EMC 3074 © Evan-Moor Corp.	Units of Length EMC 3074 © Evan-Moor Corp.	Units of Length EMC 3074 © Evan-Moor Corp.

Take It to Your Seat Centers

Build and Use a Line Plot

Skill: Organize, display, and interpret data on a line plot

Steps to Follow

1. **Prepare the center.** (See page 3.)
2. **Introduce the center.** State the goal. Say: *You will build a line plot and answer questions about the data.*
3. **Teach the skill.** Demonstrate how to use the center with individual students or small groups.
4. **Practice the skill.** Have students use the center independently or with a partner.

Contents

Name ______________________ Skill: Organize, display, and interpret data on a line plot

Build and Use a Line Plot

Look at the mat. Use the line plot to answer the questions below.

1. What question did Jake probably ask his classmates to get his data?

   ____

2. How many classmates did Jake survey? __________

3. How many pets do most of his classmates have? __________

4. How many classmates have no pets? __________

5. How many classmates have more than five pets? __________

6. How many more classmates have two pets than five pets? __________

7. Is the total number of classmates with three, four, and five pets more or less than the number of classmates with two pets? ______________

8. What is the total number of classmates with the most pets and with only one pet? __________

9. How many pets in all do Jake's classmates have? __________

10. How can you tell whether more classmates have five pets or six pets?

    ____

11. How many of Jake's classmates have the same number of pets you do? __________

Build and Use a Line Plot

Skill: Organize, display, and interpret data on a line plot

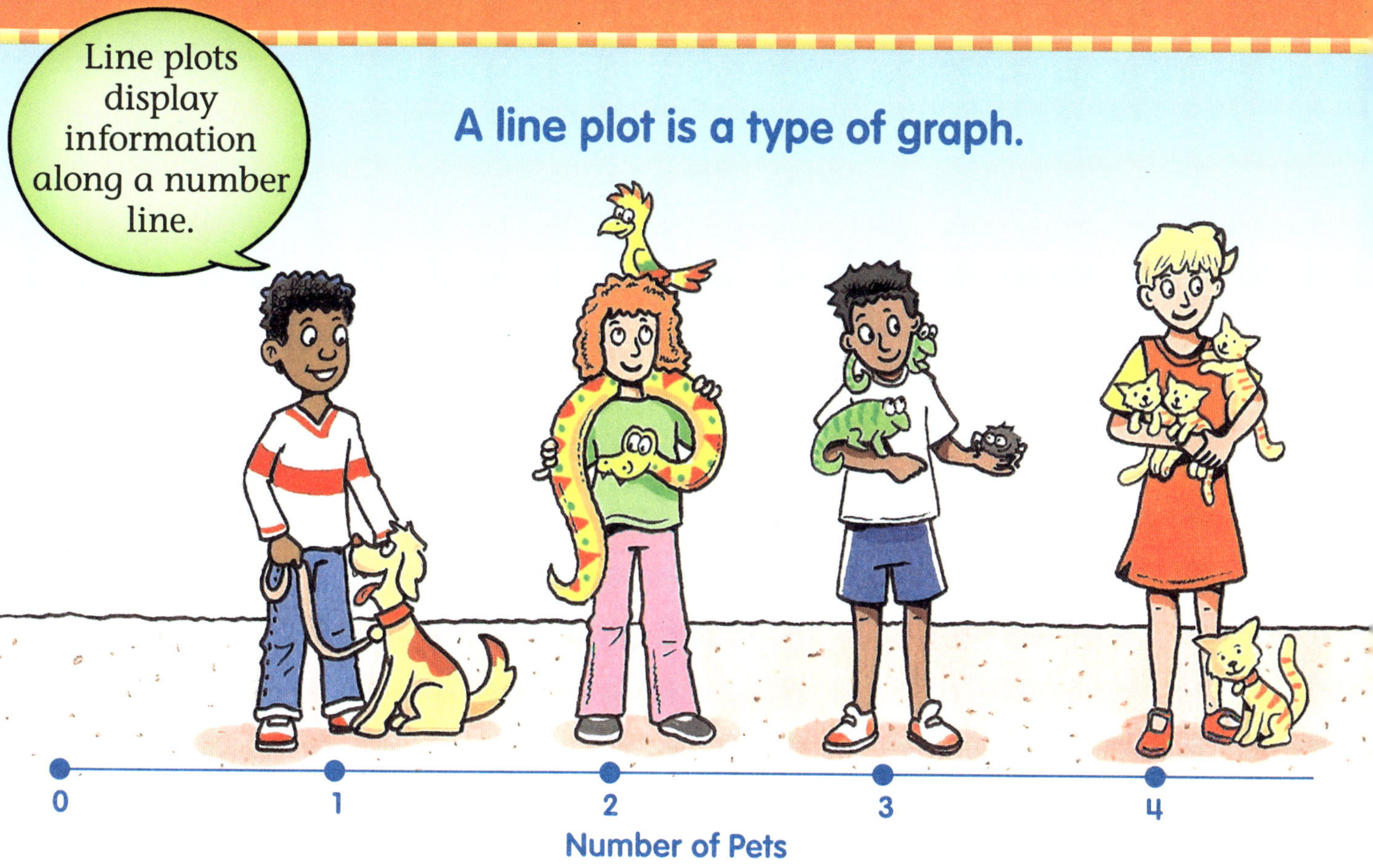

Line plots display information along a number line.
A line plot is a type of graph.
0
1
2
3
4
Number of Pets

1. Lay out the mat and the cards.
2. Read the information at the top of the mat and review the data chart.
3. Place **X** cards above the numbers along the bottom of the mat to plot the data from the chart.
4. Use your line plot to answer the questions on the response form.

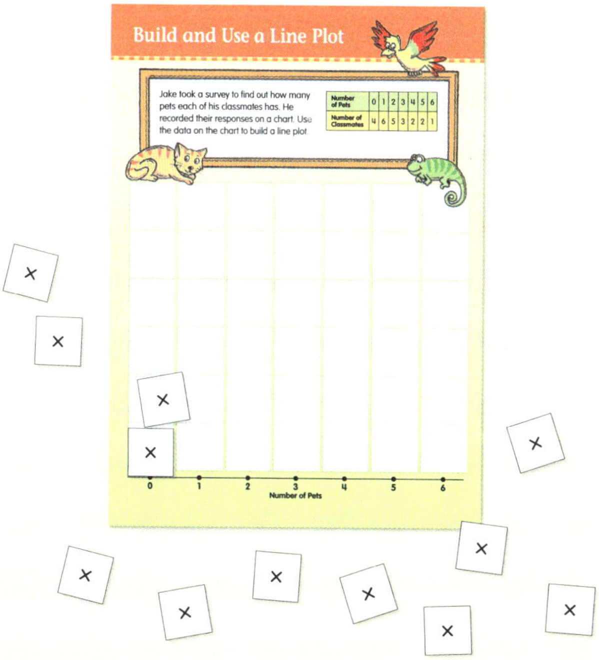

Build and Use a Line Plot

Answer Key

(fold)

Response Form

Build and Use a Line Plot

Look at the mat. Use the line plot to answer the questions below.

1. What question did Jake probably ask his classmates to get his data? How many pets do you have?
2. How many classmates did Jake survey? 23
3. How many pets do most of his classmates have? 1
4. How many classmates have no pets? 4
5. How many classmates have more than five pets? 1
6. How many more classmates have two pets than five pets? 3
7. Is the total number of classmates with three, four, and five pets more or less than the number of classmates with two pets? more
8. What is the total number of classmates with the most pets and with only one pet? 7
9. How many pets in all do Jake's classmates have? 53
10. How can you tell whether more classmates have five pets or six pets? You count the **X**s.
11. How many of Jake's classmates have the same number of pets you do? ______

Answers will vary.

Answer Key

Build and Use a Line Plot

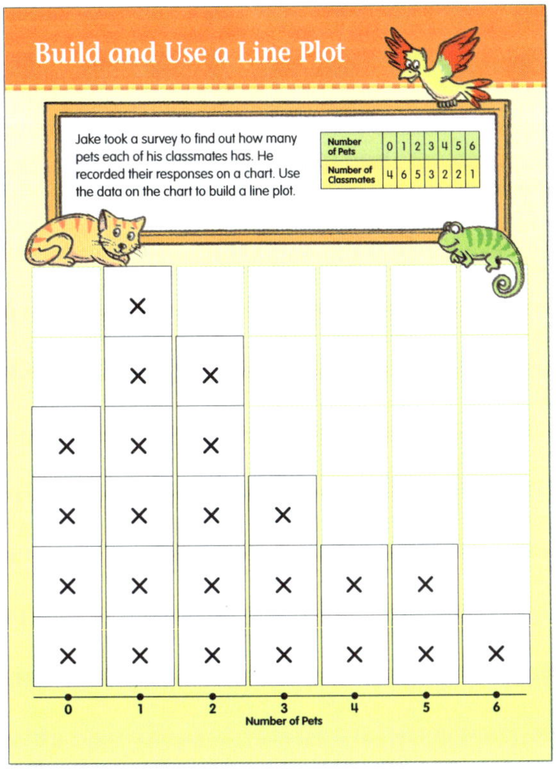

Build and Use a Line Plot

Jake took a survey to find out how many pets each of his classmates has. He recorded their responses on a chart. Use the data on the chart to build a line plot.

Number of Pets	0	1	2	3	4	5	6
Number of Classmates	4	6	5	3	2	2	1

Build and Use a Line Plot

Jake took a survey to find out how many pets each of his classmates has. He recorded their responses on a chart. Use the data on the chart to build a line plot.

Number of Pets	0	1	2	3	4	5	6
Number of Classmates	4	6	5	3	2	2	1

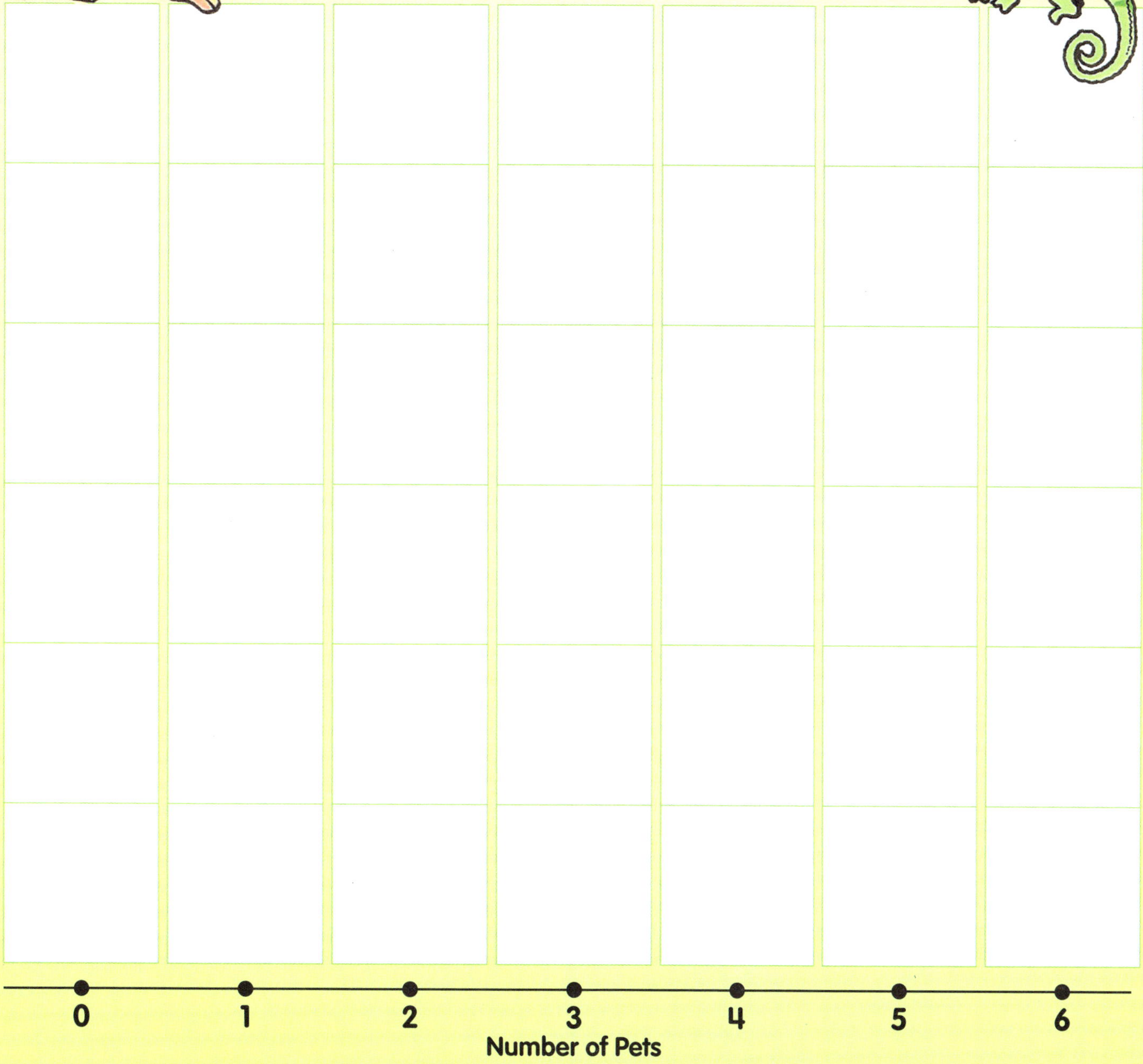

×	×	×	×	×	×	×
×	×	×	×	×	×	×
×	×	×	×	×	×	×
×	×	×	×	×	×	×
×	×	×	×	×	×	×

Build and Use a Line Plot EMC 3074 © Evan-Moor Corp.	Build and Use a Line Plot EMC 3074 © Evan-Moor Corp.	Build and Use a Line Plot EMC 3074 © Evan-Moor Corp.	Build and Use a Line Plot EMC 3074 © Evan-Moor Corp.	Build and Use a Line Plot EMC 3074 © Evan-Moor Corp.	Build and Use a Line Plot EMC 3074 © Evan-Moor Corp.	Build and Use a Line Plot EMC 3074 © Evan-Moor Corp.
Build and Use a Line Plot EMC 3074 © Evan-Moor Corp.	Build and Use a Line Plot EMC 3074 © Evan-Moor Corp.	Build and Use a Line Plot EMC 3074 © Evan-Moor Corp.	Build and Use a Line Plot EMC 3074 © Evan-Moor Corp.	Build and Use a Line Plot EMC 3074 © Evan-Moor Corp.	Build and Use a Line Plot EMC 3074 © Evan-Moor Corp.	Build and Use a Line Plot EMC 3074 © Evan-Moor Corp.
Build and Use a Line Plot EMC 3074 © Evan-Moor Corp.	Build and Use a Line Plot EMC 3074 © Evan-Moor Corp.	Build and Use a Line Plot EMC 3074 © Evan-Moor Corp.	Build and Use a Line Plot EMC 3074 © Evan-Moor Corp.	Build and Use a Line Plot EMC 3074 © Evan-Moor Corp.	Build and Use a Line Plot EMC 3074 © Evan-Moor Corp.	Build and Use a Line Plot EMC 3074 © Evan-Moor Corp.
Build and Use a Line Plot EMC 3074 © Evan-Moor Corp.	Build and Use a Line Plot EMC 3074 © Evan-Moor Corp.	Build and Use a Line Plot EMC 3074 © Evan-Moor Corp.	Build and Use a Line Plot EMC 3074 © Evan-Moor Corp.	Build and Use a Line Plot EMC 3074 © Evan-Moor Corp.	Build and Use a Line Plot EMC 3074 © Evan-Moor Corp.	Build and Use a Line Plot EMC 3074 © Evan-Moor Corp.
Build and Use a Line Plot EMC 3074 © Evan-Moor Corp.	Build and Use a Line Plot EMC 3074 © Evan-Moor Corp.	Build and Use a Line Plot EMC 3074 © Evan-Moor Corp.	Build and Use a Line Plot EMC 3074 © Evan-Moor Corp.	Build and Use a Line Plot EMC 3074 © Evan-Moor Corp.	Build and Use a Line Plot EMC 3074 © Evan-Moor Corp.	Build and Use a Line Plot EMC 3074 © Evan-Moor Corp.

Angles

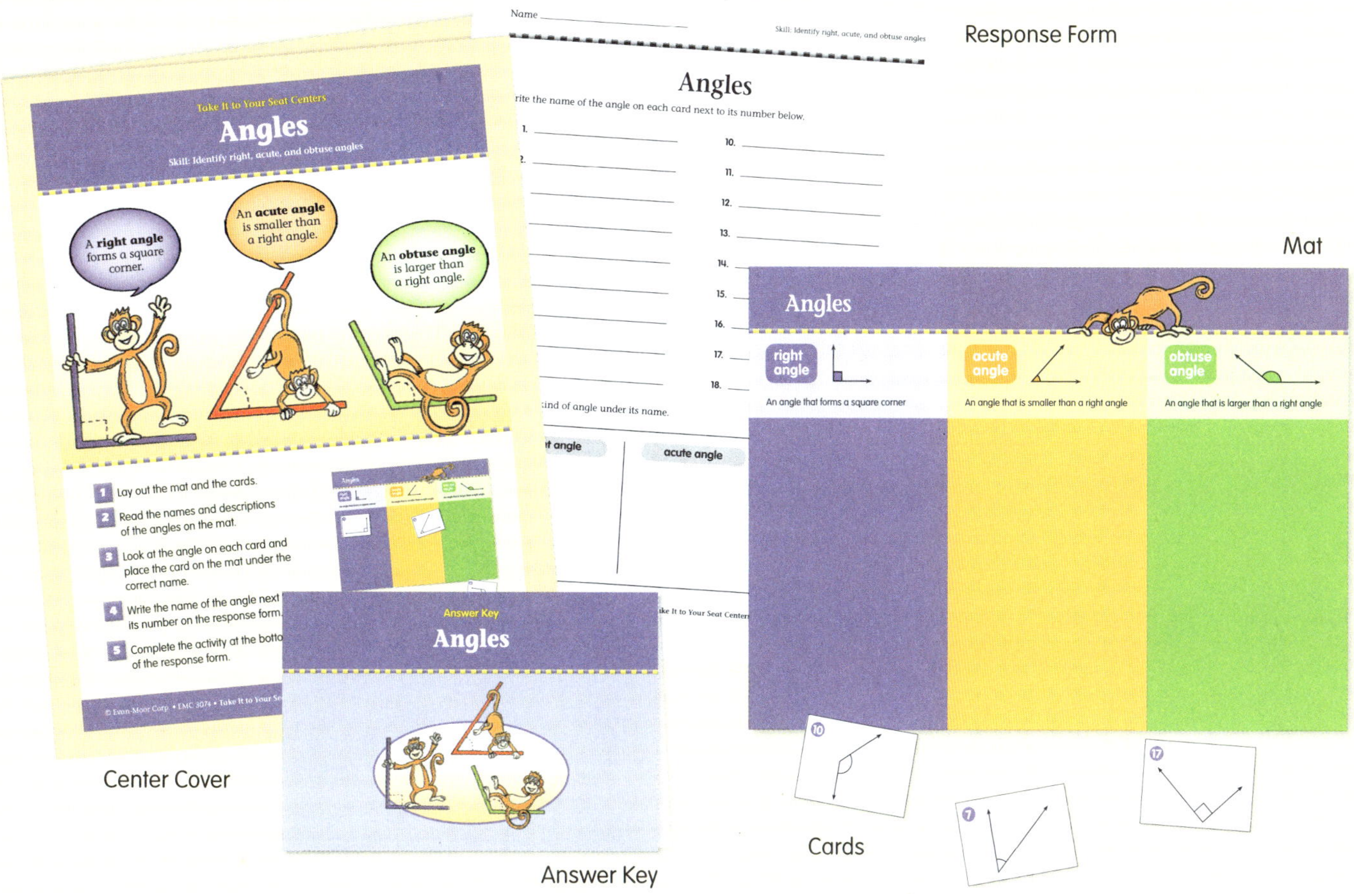

Skill: Identify right, acute, and obtuse angles

Steps to Follow

1. **Prepare the center.** (See page 3.)
2. **Introduce the center.** State the goal. Say: *You will identify the kind of angle on each card and place it in the correct section on the mat.*
3. **Teach the skill.** Demonstrate how to use the center with individual students or small groups.
4. **Practice the skill.** Have students use the center independently or with a partner.

Contents

Name ______________________________

Skill: Identify right, acute, and obtuse angles

Angles

Write the name of the angle on each card next to its number below.

1. ______________________________
2. ______________________________
3. ______________________________
4. ______________________________
5. ______________________________
6. ______________________________
7. ______________________________
8. ______________________________
9. ______________________________
10. ______________________________
11. ______________________________
12. ______________________________
13. ______________________________
14. ______________________________
15. ______________________________
16. ______________________________
17. ______________________________
18. ______________________________

Draw each kind of angle under its name.

right angle	acute angle	obtuse angle

Angles

Skill: Identify right, acute, and obtuse angles

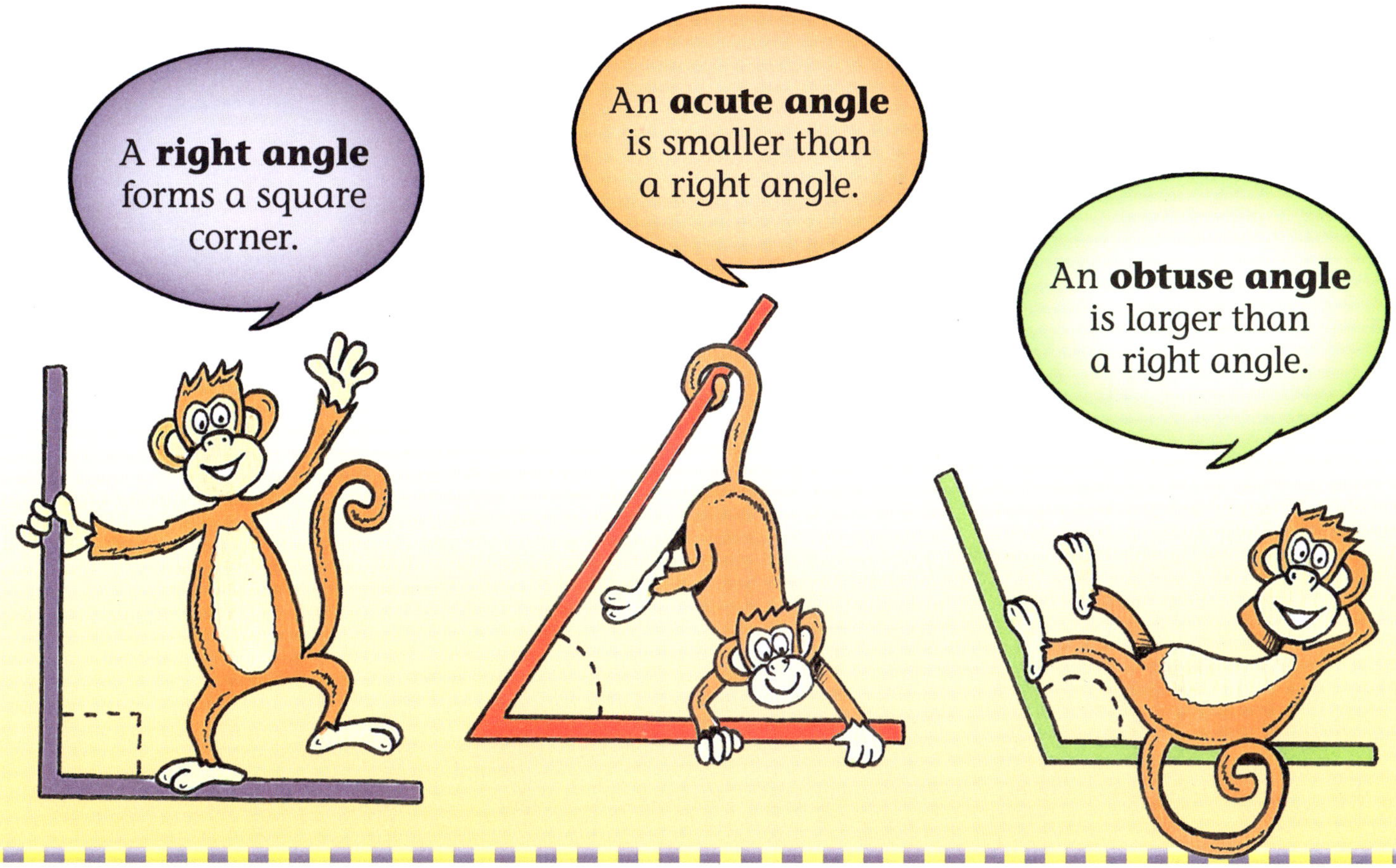

1. Lay out the mat and the cards.
2. Read the names and descriptions of the angles on the mat.
3. Look at the angle on each card and place the card on the mat under the correct name.
4. Write the name of the angle next to its number on the response form.
5. Complete the activity at the bottom of the response form.

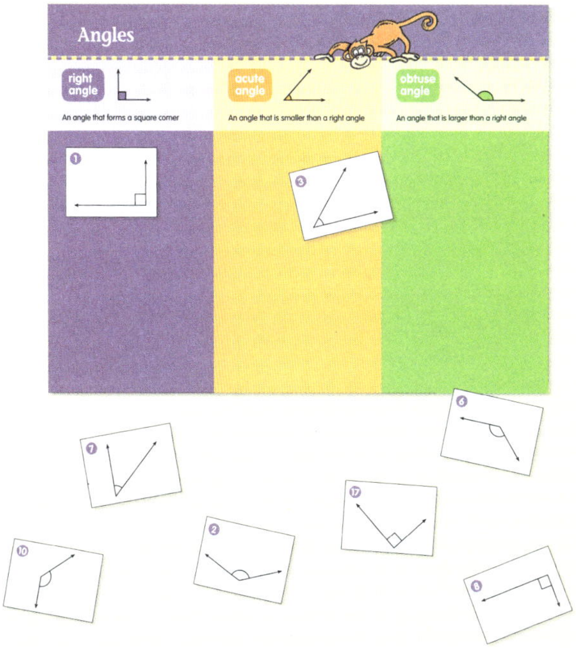

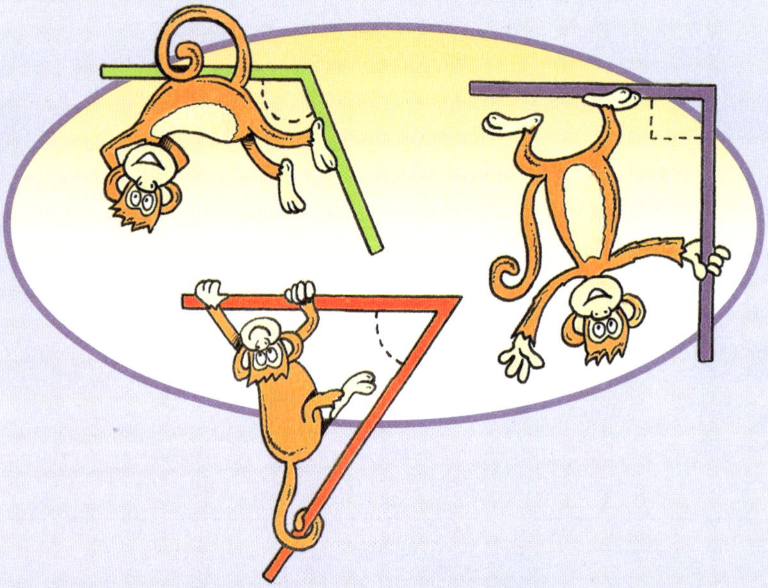

Angles

Answer Key

(fold)

Response Form

Angles

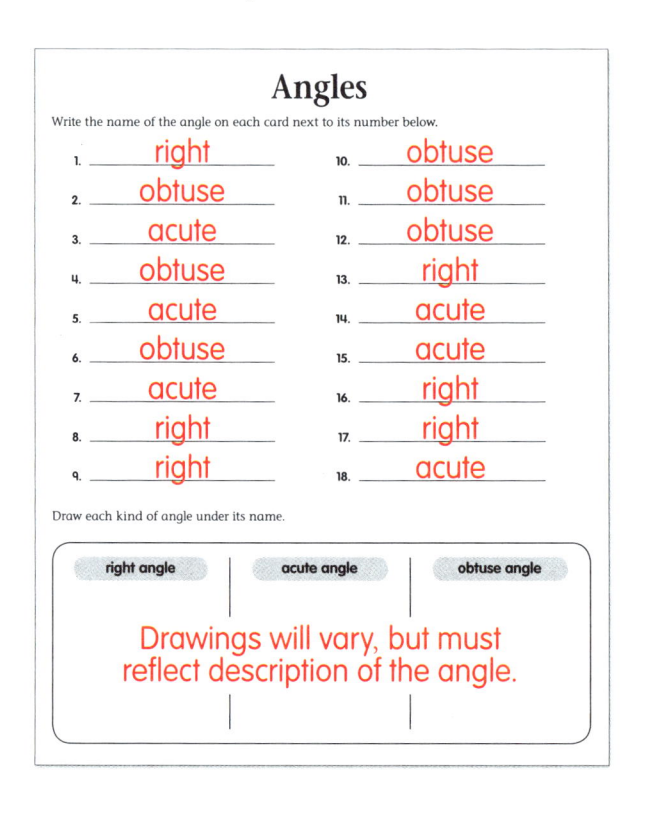

Write the name of the angle on each card next to its number below.

1.	right	10.	obtuse
2.	obtuse	11.	obtuse
3.	acute	12.	obtuse
4.	obtuse	13.	right
5.	acute	14.	acute
6.	obtuse	15.	acute
7.	acute	16.	right
8.	right	17.	right
9.	right	18.	acute

Draw each kind of angle under its name.

right angle	acute angle	obtuse angle

Drawings will vary, but must reflect description of the angle.

Answer Key

Angles

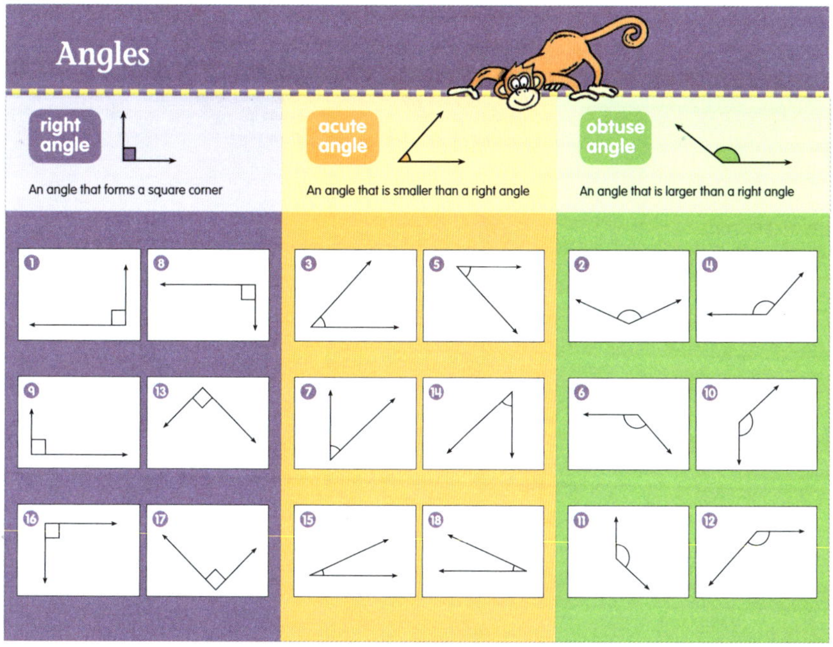

Angles

right angle

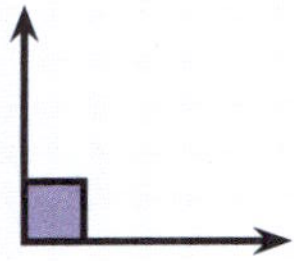

An angle that forms a square corner

acute angle

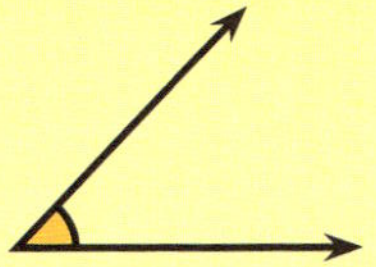

An angle that is smaller than a right angle

obtuse angle

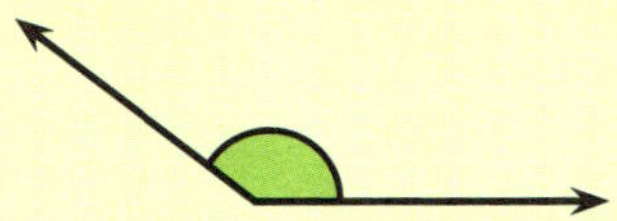

An angle that is larger than a right angle

1

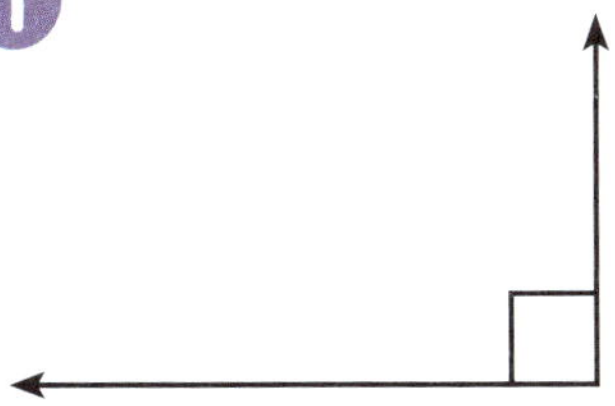

2

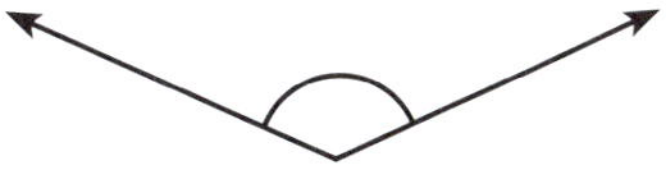

3

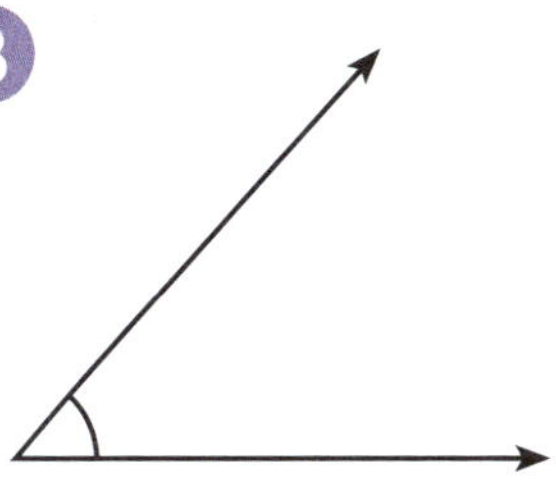

4

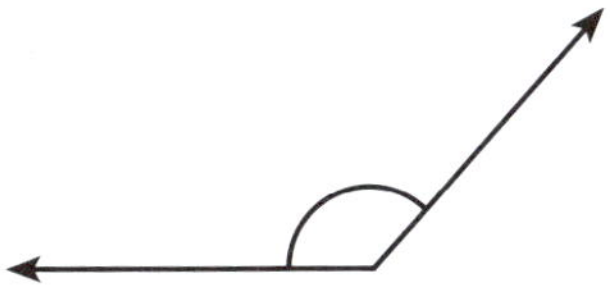

5

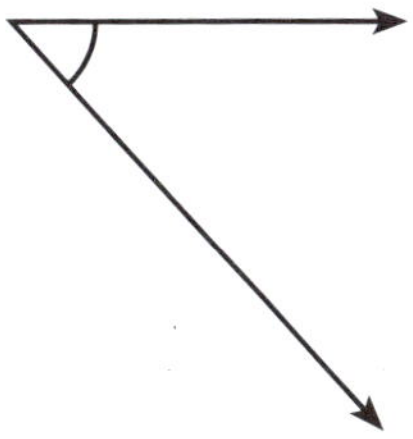

6

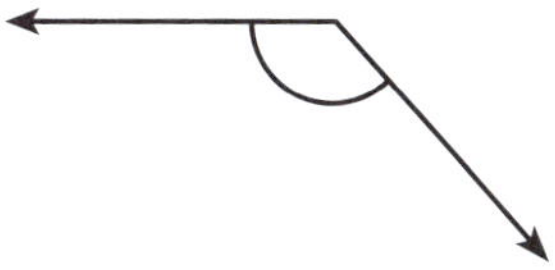

7

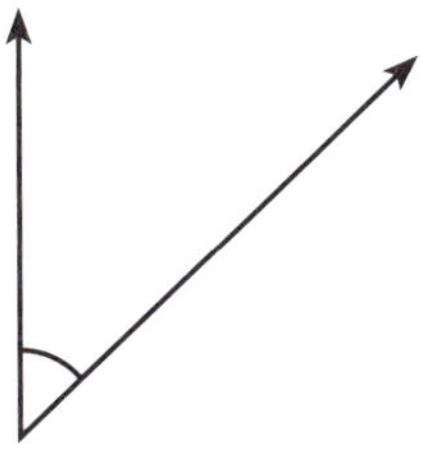

8

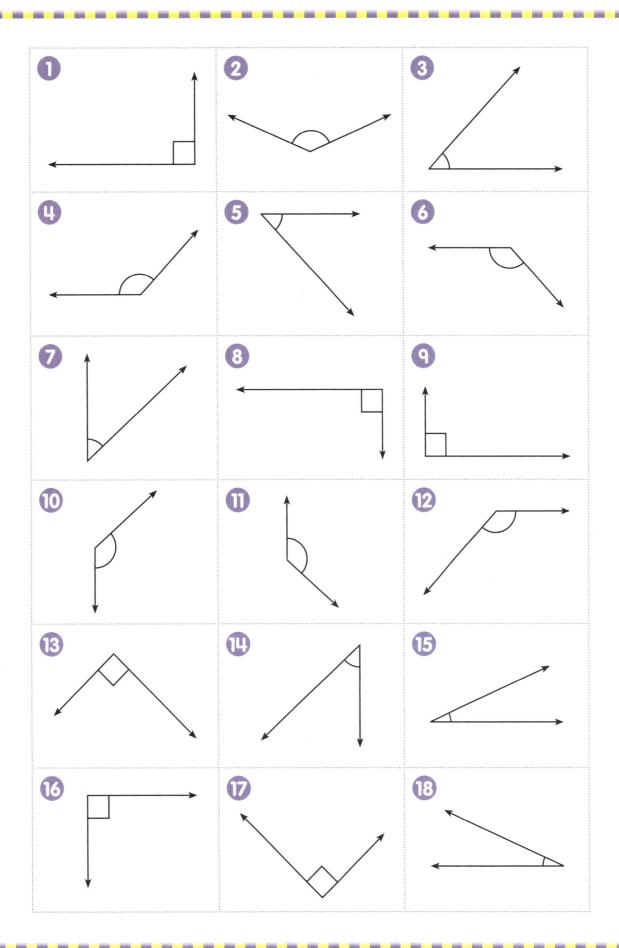

9

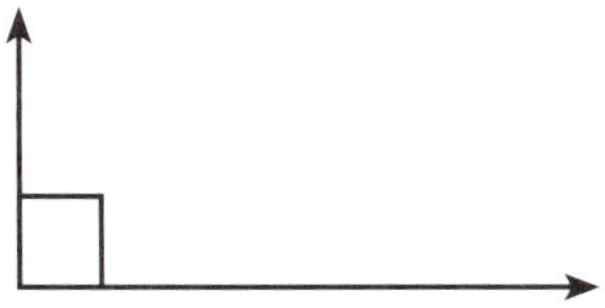

10

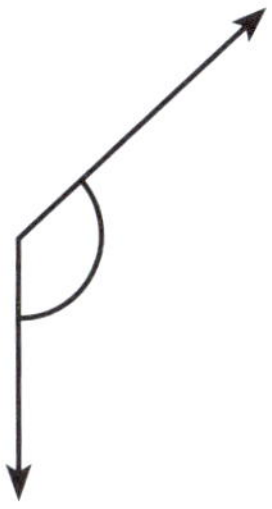

11

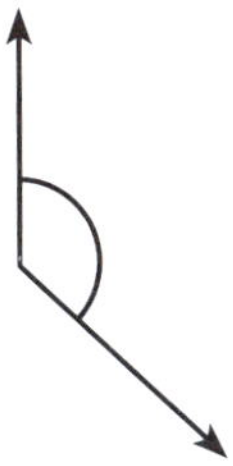

12

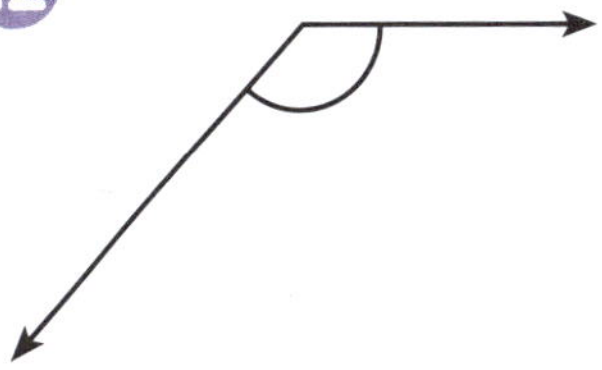

13

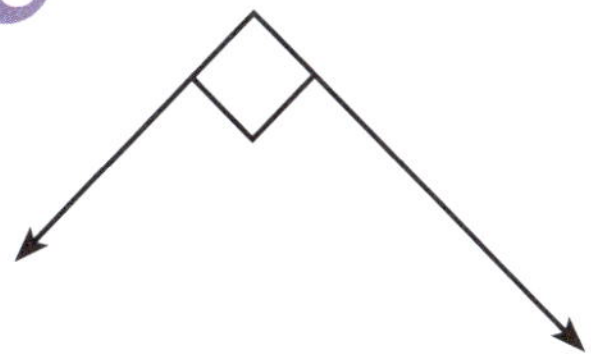

14

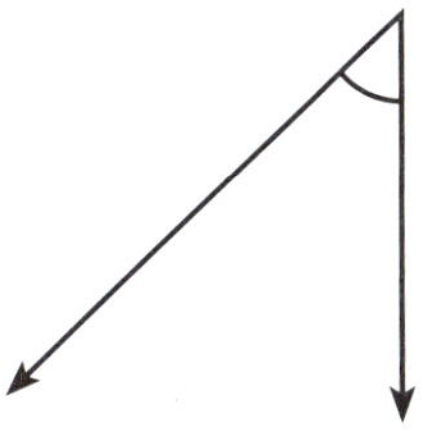

15

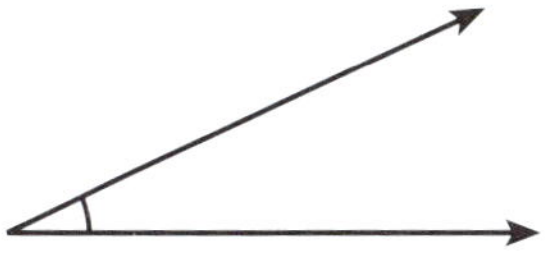

16

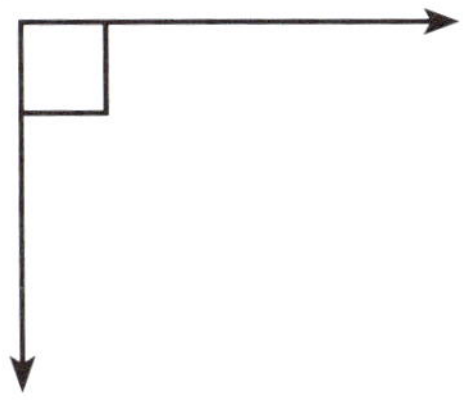

17

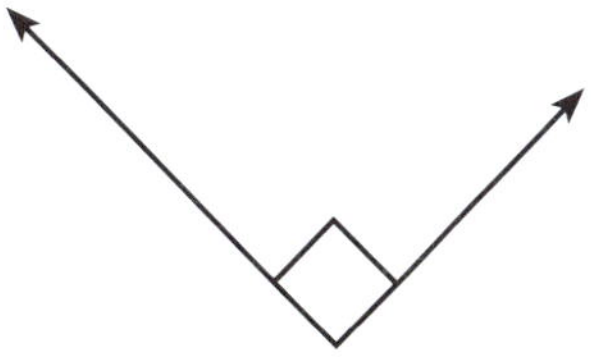

18

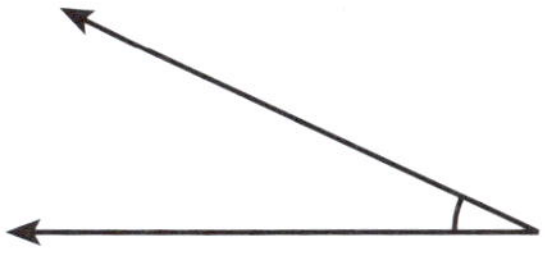

Angles
EMC 3074
© Evan-Moor Corp.

Angles
EMC 3074
© Evan-Moor Corp.

Angles
EMC 3074
© Evan-Moor Corp.

Angles
EMC 3074
© Evan-Moor Corp.

Angles
EMC 3074
© Evan-Moor Corp.

Angles
EMC 3074
© Evan-Moor Corp.

Angles
EMC 3074
© Evan-Moor Corp.

Angles
EMC 3074
© Evan-Moor Corp.

Angles
EMC 3074
© Evan-Moor Corp.

Angles
EMC 3074
© Evan-Moor Corp.

Angles
EMC 3074
© Evan-Moor Corp.

Angles
EMC 3074
© Evan-Moor Corp.

Angles
EMC 3074
© Evan-Moor Corp.

Angles
EMC 3074
© Evan-Moor Corp.

Angles
EMC 3074
© Evan-Moor Corp.

Angles
EMC 3074
© Evan-Moor Corp.

Angles
EMC 3074
© Evan-Moor Corp.

Angles
EMC 3074
© Evan-Moor Corp.

Take It to Your Seat Centers

Words and Terms

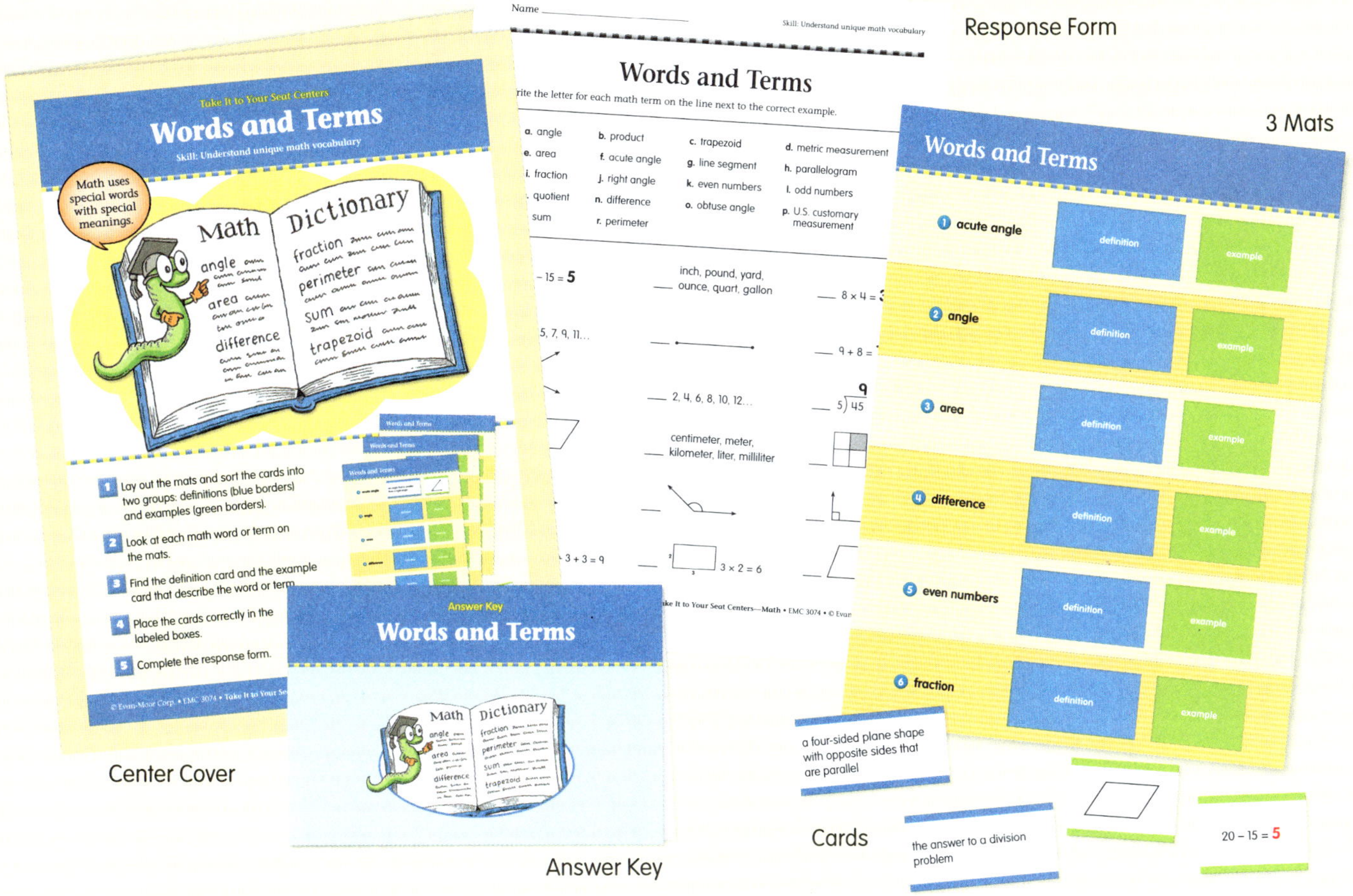

Skill: Understand unique math vocabulary

Steps to Follow

1. **Prepare the center.** (See page 3.)
2. **Introduce the center.** State the goal. Say: *You will match math words and terms with definitions and examples to show how much math vocabulary you know.*
3. **Teach the skill.** Demonstrate how to use the center with individual students or small groups.
4. **Practice the skill.** Have students use the center independently or with a partner.

Contents

Words and Terms

Write the letter for each math term on the line next to the correct example.

a. angle	**b.** product	**c.** trapezoid	**d.** metric measurement
e. area	**f.** acute angle	**g.** line segment	**h.** parallelogram
i. fraction	**j.** right angle	**k.** even numbers	**l.** odd numbers
m. quotient	**n.** difference	**o.** obtuse angle	**p.** U.S. customary measurement
q. sum	**r.** perimeter		

n 20 – 15 = **5**

___ inch, pound, yard, ounce, quart, gallon

___ 8 × 4 = **32**

___ 1, 3, 5, 7, 9, 11...

___

___ 9 + 8 = **17**

___ 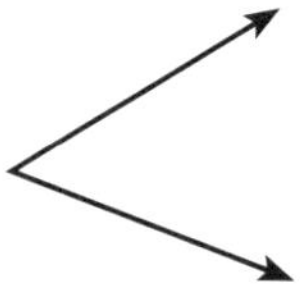

___ 2, 4, 6, 8, 10, 12...

___ $\begin{array}{r} \mathbf{9} \\ 5\overline{)45} \end{array}$

___ 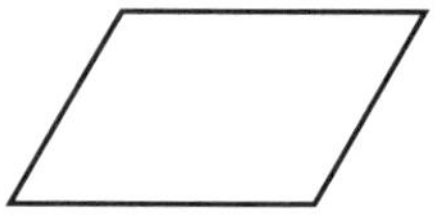

___ centimeter, meter, kilometer, liter, milliliter

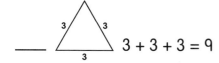

___ 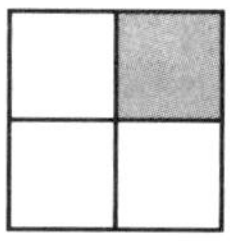 $\frac{1}{4}$

___ 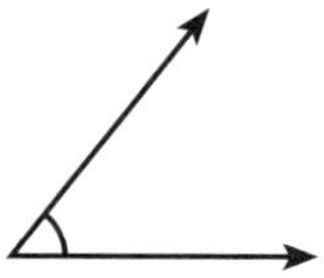

___ 

___ 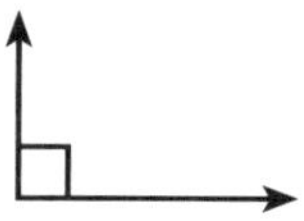

___ 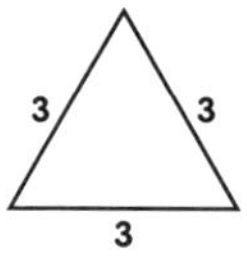

3 + 3 + 3 = 9

___ 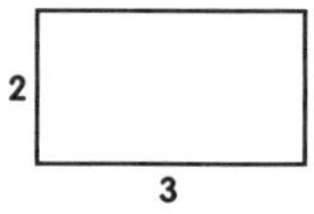

3 × 2 = 6

___ 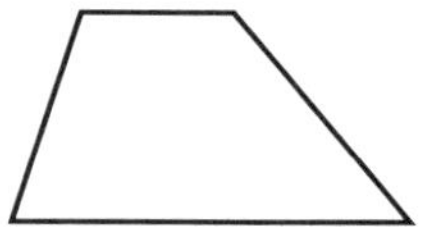

Take It to Your Seat Centers

Words and Terms

Skill: Understand unique math vocabulary

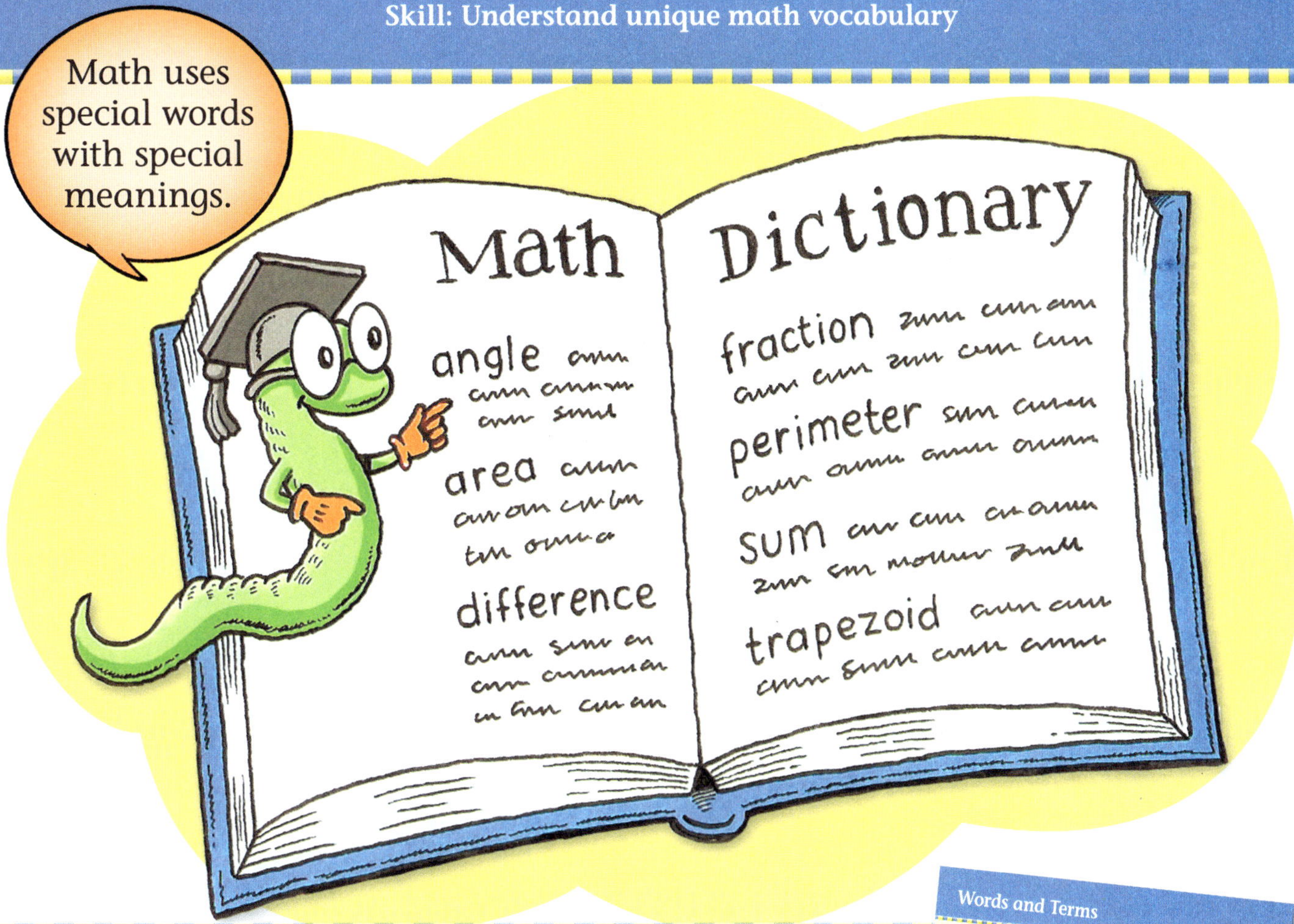

1. Lay out the mats and sort the cards into two groups: definitions (blue borders) and examples (green borders).
2. Look at each math word or term on the mats.
3. Find the definition card and the example card that describe the word or term.
4. Place the cards correctly in the labeled boxes.
5. Complete the response form.

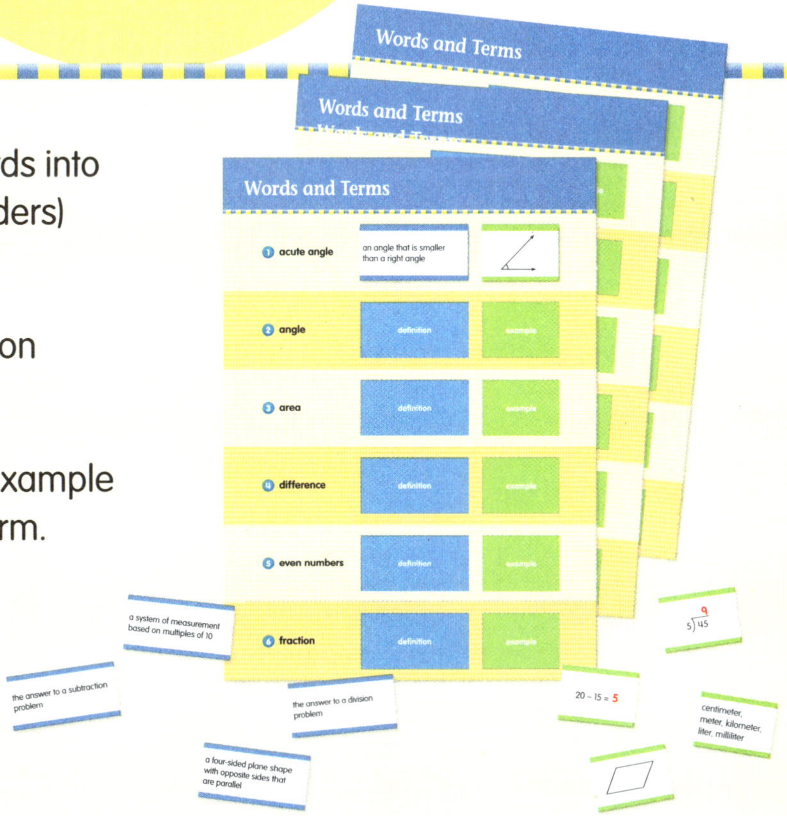

Words and Terms

Answer Key

(fold)

Response Form

Words and Terms

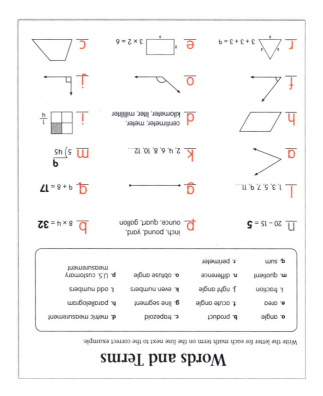

Write the letter for each math term on the line next to the correct example.

a. angle	**b.** product	**c.** trapezoid	**d.** metric measurement
e. area	**f.** acute angle	**g.** line segment	**h.** parallelogram
i. fraction	**j.** right angle	**k.** even numbers	**l.** odd numbers
m. quotient	**n.** difference	**o.** obtuse angle	**p.** U.S. customary measurement
q. sum	**r.** perimeter		

n 20 − 15 = **5**	p inch, pound, yard, ounce, quart, gallon	b 8 × 4 = **32**
l 1, 3, 5, 7, 9, 11...	g	q 9 + 8 = **17**
a	k 2, 4, 6, 8, 10, 12...	m $5\overline{)45}$ = **9**
h	d centimeter, meter, kilometer, liter, milliliter	i $\frac{1}{4}$
f	o	j
r 3 + 3 + 3 = 9	e 3 × 2 = 6	c

Answer Key

Words and Terms

Words and Terms

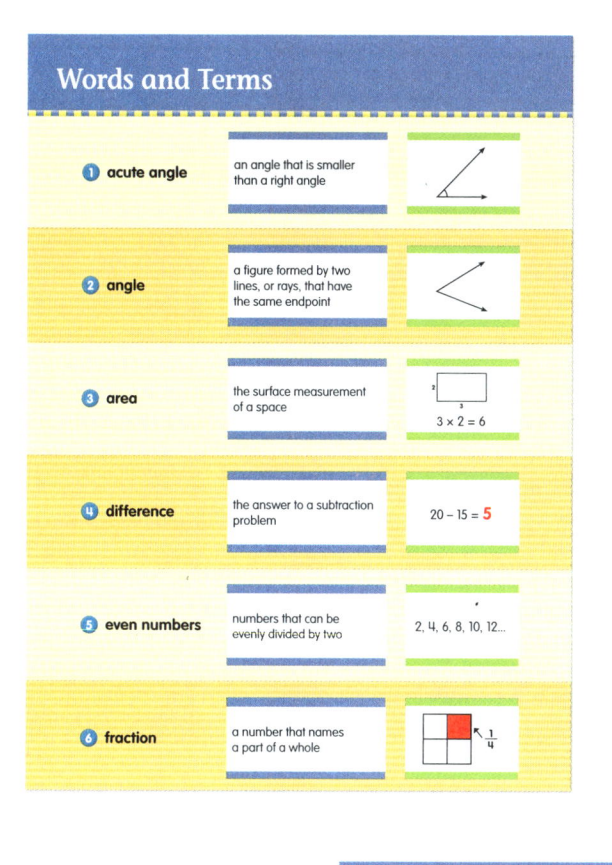

1 **acute angle**	an angle that is smaller than a right angle	
2 **angle**	a figure formed by two lines, or rays, that have the same endpoint	
3 **area**	the surface measurement of a space	 $3 \times 2 = 6$
4 **difference**	the answer to a subtraction problem	$20 - 15 = 5$
5 **even numbers**	numbers that can be evenly divided by two	2, 4, 6, 8, 10, 12...
6 **fraction**	a number that names a part of a whole	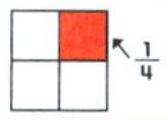

Words and Terms

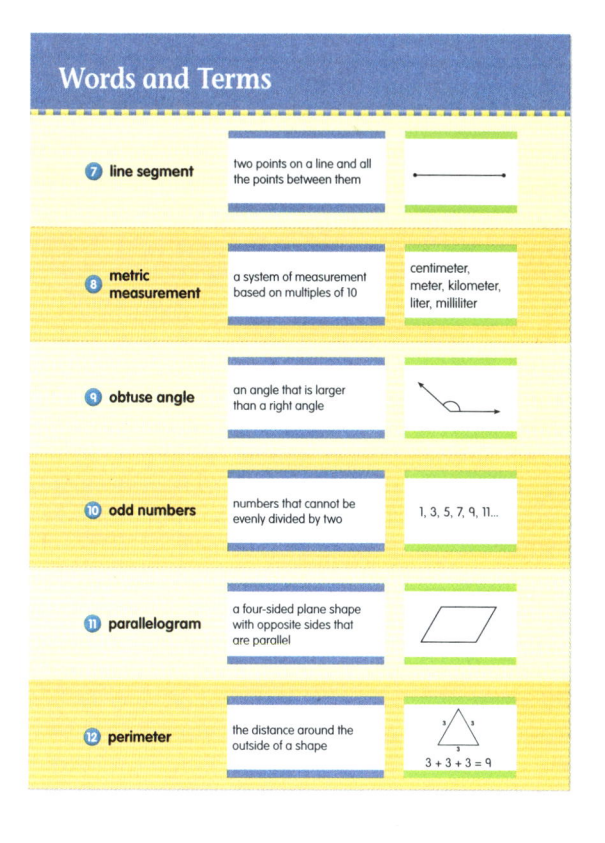

7 **line segment**	two points on a line and all the points between them	
8 **metric measurement**	a system of measurement based on multiples of 10	centimeter, meter, kilometer, liter, milliliter
9 **obtuse angle**	an angle that is larger than a right angle	
10 **odd numbers**	numbers that cannot be evenly divided by two	1, 3, 5, 7, 9, 11...
11 **parallelogram**	a four-sided plane shape with opposite sides that are parallel	
12 **perimeter**	the distance around the outside of a shape	 $3 + 3 + 3 = 9$

Words and Terms

13 **product**	the answer to a multiplication problem	$8 \times 4 = 32$
14 **quotient**	the answer to a division problem	$45 \div 5 = 9$
15 **right angle**	an angle that forms a square corner	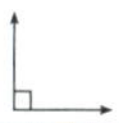
16 **sum**	the answer to an addition problem	$9 + 8 = 17$
17 **trapezoid**	a four-sided plane shape with two parallel sides and two sides that are not parallel	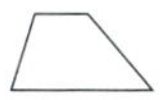
18 **U.S. customary measurement**	units of measure used in the United States	inch, pound, yard, ounce, quart, gallon

Words and Terms

1 acute angle	definition	example
2 angle	definition	example
3 area	definition	example
4 difference	definition	example
5 even numbers	definition	example
6 fraction	definition	example

Words and Terms

7 line segment	definition	example
8 metric measurement	definition	example
9 obtuse angle	definition	example
10 odd numbers	definition	example
11 parallelogram	definition	example
12 perimeter	definition	example

Words and Terms

13 product	definition	example
14 quotient	definition	example
15 right angle	definition	example
16 sum	definition	example
17 trapezoid	definition	example
18 U.S. customary measurement	definition	example

a figure formed by two lines, or rays, that have the same endpoint	two points on a line and all the points between them	the answer to a division problem
numbers that cannot be evenly divided by two	numbers that can be evenly divided by two	the answer to an addition problem
the answer to a multiplication problem	a number that names a part of a whole	a system of measurement based on multiples of 10
the surface measurement of a space	a four-sided plane shape with opposite sides that are parallel	an angle that is smaller than a right angle
an angle that forms a square corner	a four-sided plane shape with two parallel sides and two sides that are not parallel	units of measure used in the United States
an angle that is larger than a right angle	the distance around the outside of a shape	the answer to a subtraction problem

Words and Terms

EMC 3074
© Evan-Moor Corp.

Words and Terms

EMC 3074
© Evan-Moor Corp.

Words and Terms

EMC 3074
© Evan-Moor Corp.

Words and Terms

EMC 3074
© Evan-Moor Corp.

Words and Terms

EMC 3074
© Evan-Moor Corp.

Words and Terms

EMC 3074
© Evan-Moor Corp.

Words and Terms

EMC 3074
© Evan-Moor Corp.

Words and Terms

EMC 3074
© Evan-Moor Corp.

Words and Terms

EMC 3074
© Evan-Moor Corp.

Words and Terms

EMC 3074
© Evan-Moor Corp.

Words and Terms

EMC 3074
© Evan-Moor Corp.

Words and Terms

EMC 3074
© Evan-Moor Corp.

Words and Terms

EMC 3074
© Evan-Moor Corp.

Words and Terms

EMC 3074
© Evan-Moor Corp.

Words and Terms

EMC 3074
© Evan-Moor Corp.

Words and Terms

EMC 3074
© Evan-Moor Corp.

Words and Terms

EMC 3074
© Evan-Moor Corp.

Words and Terms

EMC 3074
© Evan-Moor Corp.

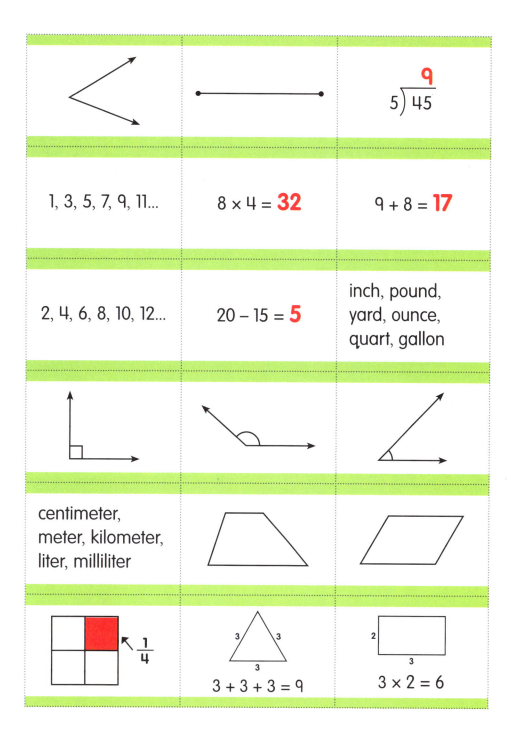

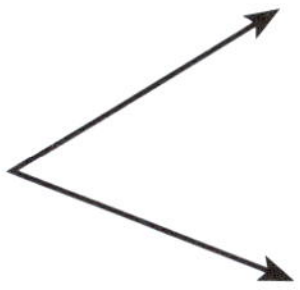		$\begin{array}{r}9\\5\overline{)45}\end{array}$
1, 3, 5, 7, 9, 11...	$8 \times 4 =$ **32**	$9 + 8 =$ **17**
2, 4, 6, 8, 10, 12...	$20 - 15 =$ **5**	inch, pound, yard, ounce, quart, gallon
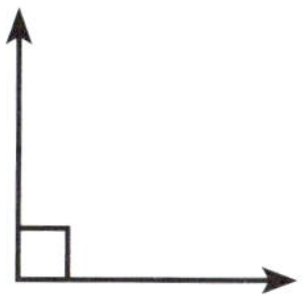		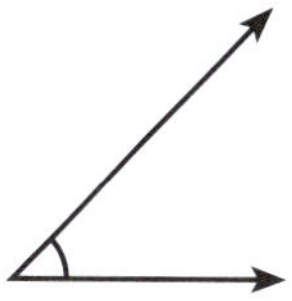
centimeter, meter, kilometer, liter, milliliter	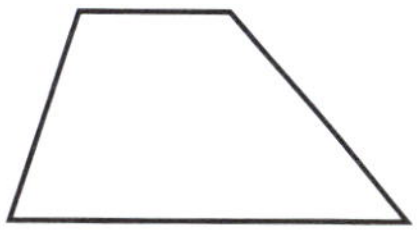	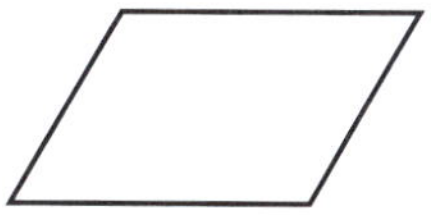
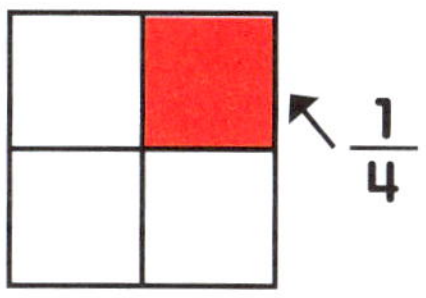	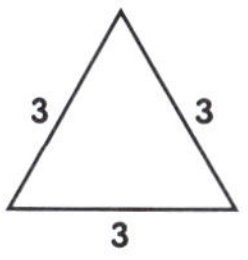 $3 + 3 + 3 = 9$	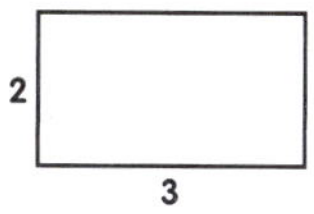 $3 \times 2 = 6$

Words and Terms EMC 3074 © Evan-Moor Corp.	**Words and Terms** EMC 3074 © Evan-Moor Corp.	**Words and Terms** EMC 3074 © Evan-Moor Corp.
Words and Terms EMC 3074 © Evan-Moor Corp.	**Words and Terms** EMC 3074 © Evan-Moor Corp.	**Words and Terms** EMC 3074 © Evan-Moor Corp.
Words and Terms EMC 3074 © Evan-Moor Corp.	**Words and Terms** EMC 3074 © Evan-Moor Corp.	**Words and Terms** EMC 3074 © Evan-Moor Corp.
Words and Terms EMC 3074 © Evan-Moor Corp.	**Words and Terms** EMC 3074 © Evan-Moor Corp.	**Words and Terms** EMC 3074 © Evan-Moor Corp.
Words and Terms EMC 3074 © Evan-Moor Corp.	**Words and Terms** EMC 3074 © Evan-Moor Corp.	**Words and Terms** EMC 3074 © Evan-Moor Corp.
Words and Terms EMC 3074 © Evan-Moor Corp.	**Words and Terms** EMC 3074 © Evan-Moor Corp.	**Words and Terms** EMC 3074 © Evan-Moor Corp.

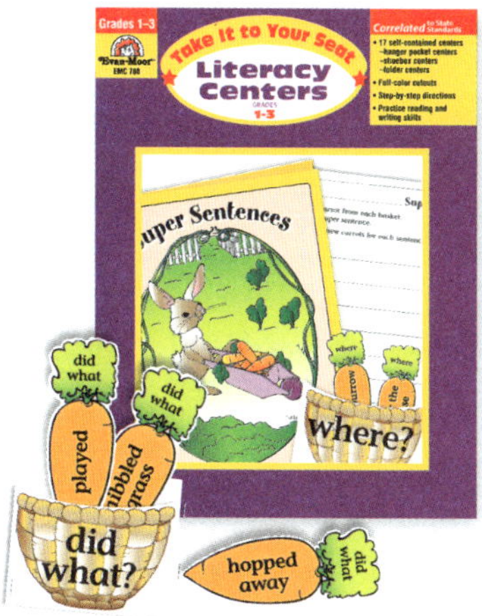

Literacy Centers

GRADES PreK–6

Add some creativity to your literacy practice with hanger pocket, shoe box, and folder centers! Each full-color literacy center uses a motivating theme and full-color materials to get your students involved in literacy practice! 192 full-color pages.

PreK–K*	EMC 2401	**Grades 3–4**	EMC 2124
Grades K–1	EMC 2123	**Grades 4–5**	EMC 2724
Grades 1–3	EMC 788	**Grades 4–6**	EMC 2719
Grades 2–3	EMC 2723		

Includes language arts and math centers

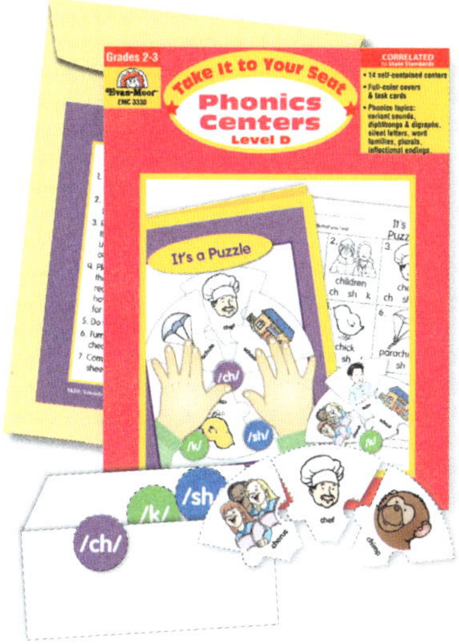

Phonics Centers

GRADES PreK–3

Hands-on phonics practice that students love! Fun, game-like formats and full-color task cards create the perfect tool to teach your students valuable phonics skills, such as rhyming words, initial and final consonant sounds, consonant blends, and more! 192 full-color pages.

PreK–K	**Level A**	EMC 3327
Grades K–1	**Level B**	EMC 3328
Grades 1–2	**Level C**	EMC 3329
Grades 2–3	**Level D**	EMC 3330

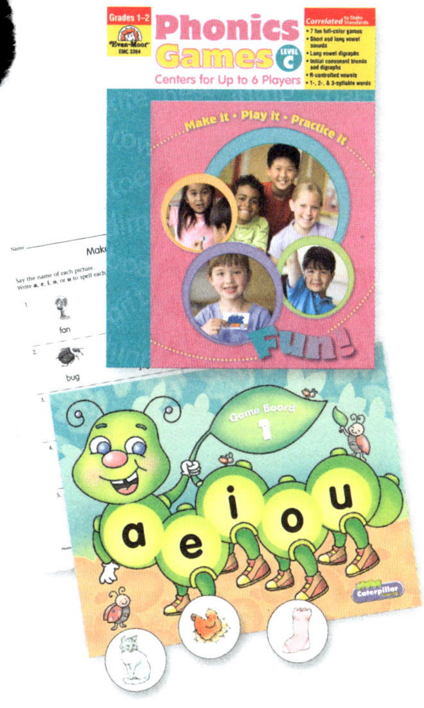

Phonics Games

Centers for Up to 6 Players

GRADES PreK–3

Each *Phonics Games* title covers the same skills as the corresponding *Basic Phonics Skills* book in a fun, hands-on format. Move through Levels A through D to sequentially practice phonics skills, beginning with phonemic awareness and ending with structural analysis, or pick the games that address your students' needs. The 7 colorful, engaging games inspire students at every level! 144 full-color pages.

Grades PreK–K	Level A	EMC 3362
Grades K–1	Level B	EMC 3363
Grades 1–2	Level C	EMC 3364
Grades 2–3	Level D	EMC 3365

Grade 2

Reading and Language Centers

GRADES K–6+

Engage your students in reading and language skills practice! The full-color centers in each ALL NEW *Take It to Your Seat Reading and Language Centers* title cover skills such as sequencing, predicting, distinguishing between real and make-believe, and more! 160 pages.

Grade K	EMC 2840	**Grade 4**	EMC 2844
Grade 1	EMC 2841	**Grade 5**	EMC 2845
Grade 2	EMC 2842	**Grade 6+**	EMC 2846
Grade 3	EMC 2843		

Grades 2–3

> *"I love that* **Take It to Your Seat Learning Centers** *have hands-on learning activities followed by a paper-and-pencil activity. They're simply the best!"*
>
> *–Sandy O.*
> *Second Grade Teacher*

Writing Centers

GRADES 1–6

Help students practice writing strong sentences & paragraphs, stories & poems, notes & letters, and more! Writing tips, models, prompts, and word banks help guide students through the entire writing process. 192 full-color pages.

Grades 1–2 EMC 6002
Grades 2–3 EMC 6003
Grades 3–4 EMC 6004
Grades 4–5 EMC 6005
Grades 5–6 EMC 6006

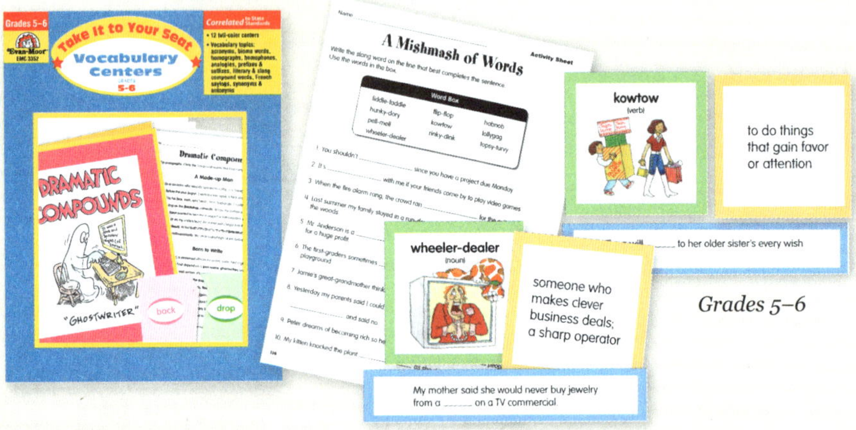

Grades 5–6

Vocabulary Centers

GRADES K–6

Engage your students as they build vocabulary and practice important skills such as analogies, prefixes and suffixes, synonyms, and more! 192 full-color pages.

Grades K–1 EMC 3347
Grades 1–2 EMC 3348
Grades 2–3 EMC 3349
Grades 3–4 EMC 3350
Grades 4–5 EMC 3351
Grades 5–6 EMC 3352

Grades PreK–K

Science Centers

GRADES PreK–4

Science Centers cover grade-level science concepts. 192 full-color pages.

Grades PreK–K EMC 5004
Grades 1–2 EMC 5002
Grades 3–4 EMC 5003

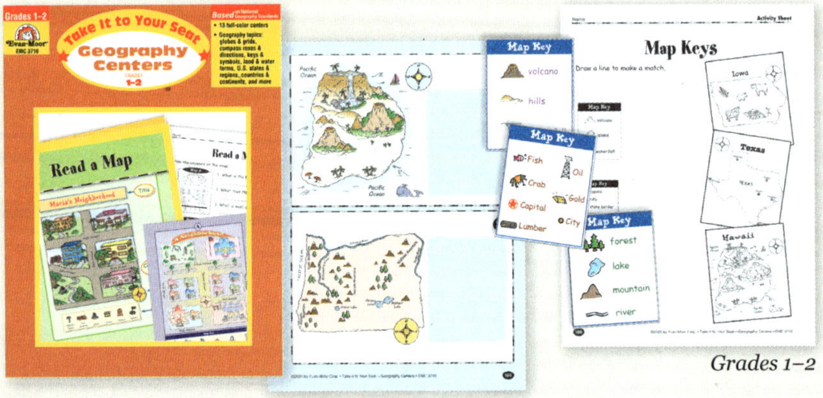

Grades 1–2

Geography Centers

GRADES 1–5

Help students practice geography vocabulary and concepts. 192 full-color pages.

Grades 1–2 EMC 3716
Grades 2–3 EMC 3717
Grades 3–4 EMC 3718
Grades 4–5 EMC 3719